CW00821076

Copyright

Create Space Edition.

ISBN-13: 978-1495409691
ISBN-10: 1495409694

excess baggage

a new kind of monasicism

Don Egan

There is often a much simpler way of doing things - if you make the effort to look for it. Simplicity does not just happen.

Edward de Bono

By the same author

The Chronicles of Godfrey

Searching for Home - a journey of the soul.

Beautiful on the Mountains – an autobiography.

Healing is coming!

Contents

'Stand at the crossroads and look; ask for the ancient paths, ask where the good way is, and walk in it, and you will find rest for your souls.'

Jeremiah 6:16

one

Huh?

For the last decade at least, there has been a silent exodus going on. The numbers are staggering. People are leaving churches of every shape and size and denomination. They are leaving in droves. Generally the church has called them 'backsliders' or said they had lost their faith. And the church carried on, seeking new members and ignoring those who left.

The vast majority of these people are not 'backsliders' nor have they lost their faith. Indeed, it is because their walk with Jesus means so much to them, that they have gone off to seek a more authentic and genuine way of being followers of Christ.

These people are exploring new ways of Christian community outside the structures of organised or institutional church. They are mostly seeking to recover something of the First Century Church – a simplicity of community, of lifestyle and worship.

This exodus has reached epic proportions. The 'de-churched' as these people have become known, now outnumber church going Christians in the UK by 2:1.

In 2011, frustrated with so many aspects of organised church, I myself went on a journey beyond the churchyard. I did not 'backslide' nor did I lose my faith. I have not joined the New Age movement. I have not started my own religion.

What I have been doing is trying to discover how to live the Christian life more like the Early Church – without the pagan influences introduced by the Emperor Constantine, and without the American business model type church.

This book is about my journey into a new simplicity and exploring the idea of a new kind of monasticism. This journey was not carried out alone. It began in conversation with a friend who has been on this journey a little longer. It has involved several friends and strangers along the way who were willing to think far outside the box, and abandon the box altogether.

I began writing reflections about my journey into simplicity. I kept meeting people who shared my frustrations and I shared some of the ideas in this book with them to hopefully help them on their way.

So I have written this book, no so much to convince anyone of anything but to be a resource that will start conversations, new trains of thought and perhaps bring healing and hope to those who feel caged in by organised church.

Jesus came to set the captives free. How strange then that so many people feel trapped, frustrated and caged by the organsation we call 'church.'

'And you shall know the truth,
and the truth shall make you free.'
John 8:32

two

Just asking

In the late 1960s I was allowed to stay up a little later, with my older brothers, to watch The Invaders – an American TV series about a man who discovers aliens have landed on Earth. The paranoid American Cold War overtones were lost on my simple mind. I sat there mesmerised, wondering if aliens had actually landed on earth. We sat in front of the coal fire in our pyjamas, eyes glued to the TV screen, gripped and fearful at the same time. Every week the narrator would recap the premise of the plotline:

'The Invaders, alien beings from a dying planet. Their destination: the Earth. Their purpose: to make it their world. David Vincent has seen them. For him, it began one lost night on a lonely country road, looking for a shortcut that he never found. It began with a closed deserted diner, and a man too long without sleep to continue his journey. It began with the landing of a craft from another galaxy. Now David Vincent knows that the Invaders are here, that they have taken human form. Somehow he must convince a disbelieving world that the nightmare has already begun.'

If the same narrator were to explain the premise of my journey into spiritual simplicity, he may say something like this:

'For Don Egan, it began one lost morning on a lonely country lane, looking for a spirituality he never found. It began with a deserted church, and a man too long without peace to continue his journey. It began with the landing of a thought from another galaxy.'

For thirty or more years, Sunday mornings for me have been about going to church. Although you will not find the phrase 'going to church' anywhere in the Bible, I had assumed that is what Christians had to do on a Sunday morning. On the rare occasions I failed to show up, I always felt guilty.

I began to attend Church in the late 1970s when I discovered Christianity. On my first Sunday morning in church, I had a very deep encounter with Jesus. I had stumbled upon this amazing community of Christians who seemed to be connected to the Holy Spirit. Theirs were not hollow words of piety or songs sung out of duty. There seemed to be electricity in the air. They appeared to be able to see something or someone I could not. Everyone seemed to be free to manifest the Holy Spirit while respecting order and the community.

Quietly, under my breath, I called out to God – or was it Jesus? Or both? 'If you are real, if you are there, come into my life.'

Immediately, gently, powerfully a wave of deep love overwhelmed me, like the embrace of an angel. A certainty flowed into my being – there was a God and he loved me, unconditionally, fully and with a raging passion. To call that encounter *'being born again'* would be to understate the matter.

As the weeks past, I discovered a loving community of people who welcomed me into their lives and homes. They accepted my hippy appearance and apart from one old lady, they accepted my long hair. We discovered God together. We gave and received forgiveness, healing and genuine care. As the name of the church implied, it was a Holy Family. My wife and I were married there and two of our children baptised there.

Later on we moved to London as I began to train for full-time ministry. Then we found ourselves part of different churches where the feeling of being family seemed to be missing. Now acceptance seemed based on expectations of the community, the branch of churchmanship and shared assumptions. I found some things the church did to be strange. They seemed to be locked into using ancient buildings, jumble sales, coffee mornings and flower rotas.

Questions began to form in my mind but, out of respect for this ancient institution, I tried to answer them myself, assuming there would always be a reason for the rituals and practices, in the Bible or in church history.

Over the last three decades I have travelled across Asia, Africa and Europe, and across denominations and traditions, where I encountered churches of every shade and style – loud, garish and flamboyant worship in the Philippines; Africans singing acapella worship in the village; English monks singing monastic chants; bells and smells; simple brethren communities; Baptist brimstone; mega church rock bands and everything in between.

In terms of my own church membership I have mostly attended Anglican Churches – even being on the staff of two different churches for eleven years – and a brief spell in an independent church.

All these different churches had, and have, some wonderful people in them. They all did something impressive in the community or in the Third World or both.

The leaders all seemed to work very hard, doing long hours and 'going the second mile'. That God was, and is, at work in all of these situations I have no doubt whatsoever. It is also true that just about every Christian community I have been part of has taught me a lot about life, about God and about relationships.

However, the older I get and the longer I pursue a living faith, in a living and loving God, the questions in my mind start to get louder and more urgent.

In many Christian circles, it is the done thing to accept the answers the leadership gives, even when they are answering questions that no one is asking.

When I was on the church staff myself, I sometimes felt uncomfortable around people who would ask too many questions, specially when those questions were fundamental to the sometimes flimsy structure that held that local church community together.

I have a friend who is great at conversation. He seems to have a skill of making you feel like you're the most important person he's ever met. He does it by asking probing questions in a friendly way. He seems interested as though, when you are with him, you're the most important person at that moment.

I've often wished I had that skill of asking more questions in friendships.

I particularly notice this questioning style of conversation in the Jewish community. It is almost like every phrase has to be formed as a question if one is Jewish. Watch any Woody Allen movie or any episode of *Seinfeld*, and count the number of questions in the dialogue.

Quite how Christianity evolved into a religion that seeks to answer all questions, and end all discussion, I have no idea. To be sure, the world is not always looking for neat answers but a place where it is OK to ask questions. The gospels are shot through with dialogues with Jesus. He doesn't always give tidy answers but ones that provoke further questions. Often Jesus himself asked questions. *'What does it profit a man ...?'*

Jesus, in case you hadn't noticed, was Jewish. In Judaism, to be without questions is not a sign of faith, but of lack of depth. In his book *The Haggadah,* Rabbi Sacks writes about the Jewish fascination with asking questions.

'The Nobel prize-winning Jewish physicist Isidore Rabi once explained that his mother taught him how to be a scientist. 'Every other child would come back from school and be asked, "What did you learn today?" But my mother used to ask, instead, "Izzy, did you ask a good question today?"' In the yeshiva, the home of traditional Talmudic learning, the highest compliment a teacher can give a student is *Du fregst a gutte kasha*, 'You raise a good objection."

Rabbi Lord Jonathan Sacks - The Haggadah.

It seems to me that God purposely provokes questions. In the story of Job, the character of Job asks why so many disasters came upon him. His friends are adamant that he must have done some evil to bring this trouble upon his family but Job objects. The long conversations go on for most of the book. The story explores the subject of human suffering. Job's friends are convinced that good things happen to good people and bad things happen to bad people. Like us, Job knows that the opposite is often just as true – bad things happen to good people and vice versa. Finally, God affirms Job but his reply is not a series of neat answers – far from it. God answers Job and his friends with an avalanche of questions. God, it seems, is not threatened by questions. He asks questions and engages with those who ask questions.

'Education is not indoctrination. It is teaching a child to be curious, to wonder, reflect, enquire. The child who asks becomes a partner in the learning process. He or she is no longer a passive recipient but an active participant. To ask is to grow.'

Rabbi Lord Jonathan Sacks

Jesus told his followers that they must come as children if they are to enter the kingdom of God. Some people have suggested that he meant to come with unquestioning faith. I can only assume such people have never had a conversation with a child. Anyone who has spent even just a few hours with a small child will know that they question everything. And even when you answer them they ask another question - *'Why?'* Before long the adult is trapped answering questions as the child drills down to the root of the issue with *'Why?'* as a response to every answer. Children are not necessarily processing your answers. What they are saying is 'I'm curious. Talk to me about this thing. Tell me stories about it.' To come as a child, as Jesus suggested, is to be curious and full of questions. Asking questions is not a sin. Asking questions is the door to the kingdom of God.

So my journey into simplicity began with some deep questions. Sometimes we fear asking fundamental questions because if we pull one thread too much, the entire garment may unravel. But, if we are seeking truth, garments that easily unravel should probably be allowed to unravel. If the Emperor indeed has no clothes, someone should have spoken out before the little child did, and saved us all the days of embarrassment.

However, I think I am trying to tug at the hem of Jesus' seamless garment because I know that when we touch that, we shall be restored. If we are hanging onto the shirt-tails of mere human constructions, it is best for all concerned that they do unravel. They will never satisfy and may sometimes even do more harm than good.

David Vincent turned an unexpected corner on his journey and discovered something that many people were unaware of. Not everyone believed him or wanted to hear about his discovery. Some people thought he was nuts.

I am not writing this book to convince anyone of anything, but to share my journey so far, that those on a similar road, into simplicity of faith, may know that they are not alone. The Truth is out there.

After thirty years of 'doing faith' in a certain way, I'd assumed there was no other way. But when the life drains out of what we are doing, when the institution eclipses the vision of the Saviour, when a sacred love letter is hijacked to justify war, greed and oppression, someone has to act. We have to push over a few sacred cows and make ourselves unpopular for a season.

My journey into simplicity was not a single idea or a sudden decision, but a gradual revelation, a conversation with God that continues to this day. It began by deconstructing long held views in order to examine their foundations. Nothing was off limits. The key was that I knew God loved us. Yet somehow, we have lost the love of God and replaced it with some sort of religious franchise, a brand, a new set of rules and required rituals dreamed up by men.

The love of God I discovered all those years ago still burns in my heart. I feel it flowing out of me towards the least, the last and the lost. Like water it naturally flows to the low places and the empty spaces in the human soul.

For the love of God, I must speak out. And that is what started to move me. The church seemed to have become mired in introspection, internal politics and legal debates. Somewhere down the line, the love of God, revealed through the Carpenter from Nazareth, seems to have been replaced by a self-important organisation. I believe Jesus is leading me to lay aside every hindrance to the love of God.

Some have suggested that I have gone too far, that there is a middle ground of compromise. But I am not looking for a compromise or a 'middle ground'. I've lived on the middle ground for thirty years. Frankly, I think it stinks. I want to put off every hindrance to follow Jesus. I want to press through the crowd and touch the hem of his garment. I want to jettison everything man-made, apart from the wounds in the hands of Jesus. I knew there was something better but I was struggling to see how to take hold of it in this life. These are my first steps on the journey.

'Those who keep speaking about the sun while walking under a cloudy sky are messengers of hope, the true saints of our day'

Henri Nouwen

three

Disturbed by bovines

I am a bit nervous around cattle. One of my pleasures
in life is hiking. Walking through the countryside on
ancient footpaths, enjoying nature and fresh air. Here
and there footpaths lead across farmland. When I enter
into a field and see a herd of cows, I become a little
fearful. They are big animals. If they charge you, you
have no chance. Some attacks, reported in the newspa-
pers, have been fatal. Generally cattle remain peaceful.
If you don't bother them, they won't bother you. Or so
one hopes.

When Moses popped up Mount Sinai to have a word
with God, the people felt he was taking too long. In the
meantime they collected all the gold and melted it down
and made a golden cow and started to worship it. They
had lost patience with the Living God who wanted a
relationship with them, and so they created their own
God and worshipped that.

When Moses finally descended the mountain he
was furious that his people had exchanged the wonder
of friendship with the Living God for the worship of

an idol – a golden cow (Exodus 32). He destroyed the sacred cow and called people to follow the Living God. That habit of replacing a relationship with the Living God for worship of an idol or sacred cow goes on to this day.

For the last twenty five years I have often found myself sitting in a congregation, looking at the perform-ance playing out at the front or on the platform, and wondered to myself 'What *are* we doing?'

And the question is not an accusation against others. I have been pregnant with that same question even when I am leading the service myself or when I have been the preacher. What *are* we doing? Why are we here is this building going through what appears to be a pointless ritual?

Sometimes I'd be watching the performance and feeling like I was from another planet. I wonder what David Vincent's aliens would have made of any random church service?

Zork from the planet Blonk lands his spaceship secretly one Sunday morning. He transforms himself into human form. He approaches the strange ancient building and wonders why it wasn't demolished and rebuilt in a modern form like all the other buildings around it. He enters and sees the worship band playing a chorus. One of the instruments or singers is slightly out of tune, but it isn't that which disturbs him. Rev Thumpbucket climbs into the pulpit and, though he begins speaking about Jesus, he seems also to accuse the congregation in parts of his talk. Zork wonders why the congregation don't interrupt the speaker or have a discussion, rather than sitting through a monologue. On the planet Blonk, learning comes through discussion

'The hallmark of an authentic evangelicalism is not the uncritical repetition of old traditions, but the willingness to submit every tradition, however ancient, to fresh biblical scrutiny and, if necessary, reform.'

John Stott

and asking questions. On Blonk, there is no hierarchy so everyone is free to speak and ask questions.

Although several phrases in the sermon make him cringe, it isn't the guilt trip that disturbed Zork. Then, appearing in seeming magic robes, Rev Thumpbucket stands at a magic table, says some magic words, and the congregation, still smarting from the preacher's accusations, queue to receive a sample of some holy medicine to keep them valid until next Sunday. Zork is disturbed.

I have some sympathy with Zork. I have observed similar rituals for decades.

And often I would come home feeling angry and unsure why that was. I assumed that I was the problem. I don't really fit in and never have. I am not alone. I know many people who just don't fit into the institution of church.

There are moments where life gives you a jolt, to force you out of religious slumber. One day I was in a church service and looked down at the performance unfolding before me. A thought occurred to me. For a moment I closed my eyes. I imagined myself to be at the Last Supper. There was Jesus and his friends having a meal. Given that Jesus gives bread and wine a new meaning at this meal, it was likely a *Shabbat* meal. There were no religious trappings as such, other than traditional Jewish prayers over the bread and wine. There was not a metal cross on the dining table that night. There was no worship band. No projector or screen. No one was wearing religious robes. There was no PA system. Jesus did not draw people's attention to the notice sheet. No events were announced. There were no appeals for volunteers to help with rotas.

Jewish people break bread and share wine at the

Shabbat supper. It is a long held tradition of theirs. On that night, Jesus tore the bread and poured the wine. And then it hit me! Whatever it was Jesus had in mind when he said *'Do this in remembrance of me,'* it was not this! It was not what most Christians do every Sunday, across the land, in church buildings and rented venues.

I opened my eyes and looked at the scene before me in church. All I could see were cows – little sacred golden cows we worshipped. Somehow we seemed to have lost the simplicity of a life of walking with Jesus. We added all these little rituals, hierarchies and accessories, and then declared them very necessary and sacred. We were not to question them. And the more of these sacred cows we added to our Christianity, the more the simple love of God became eclipsed.

Christians often told me that they were spiritually dry. They longed for something – revival, a visitation, a fresh filling, some reward for bearing the heat of the day with a good attitude. Yet try finding a believer who is walking free – who knows that they are loved by the Father - and you would be searching for a long time.

And when I talk of sacred cows and rituals, I am not pointing the finger at the historical denominations. The modern independent churches have just as many sacred cows and rituals as the historic churches, they just don't write them down in a book. Rest assured, if you offend one of their sacred cows, it will be pointed out to you very quickly.

After this revelation I lived in a disturbed state for a season. I dreaded people asking me if I had *'left the church'* or that really unbiblical question *'Which church do you go to?'* I had not left *THE* church – the one that Jesus started. But the thing we do on Sunday morning

– the thing full of sacred cows – I didn't know what to do with that.

My discomfort at that time is hard to describe. I certainly could not ignore it. The constant feeling that the world-changing life of the Son of God had been reduced down to a two hour Sunday club made me want to scream. It was like drowning in shallow water. I could no longer live in the kingdom of triteness.

Sometimes we can disturb ourselves. We can worry ourselves into a disturbed state of mind. But this didn't feel like that. My conscience was clear. I was not offended by anyone or holding any personal grudge. I was trying to press through the crowd and touch the hem of Jesus' robe, if you will. I was doing what Jesus told us to do – *'Seek first the kingdom of God and His righteousness...'* (Matthew 6:33)

Sometimes God disturbs us. He makes us uncomfortable in order to bring about change. Like a grain of sand irritating an oyster, so a pearl of great beauty may be preceded by a season of discomfort.

I was happy to be proved wrong. If it was just me being a bit awkward, I was willing to repent and do what was required by Jesus. However, in the end I concluded that not only was it God himself who was disturbing me, but he was calling me to embrace the disturbance, to allow the disturbance to birth a new season, a fresh pearl of great value.

As I embraced this holy disturbance, I discovered the words of the Prayer of Sir Francis Drake, written in a letter from his ship, Elizabeth Bonaverture, lying at anchor at Cape Sakar on 17 May 1587.

Disturb us, Lord, when
We are too well pleased with ourselves,
When our dreams have come true
Because we have dreamed too little,
When we arrived safely
Because we sailed too close to the shore.

Disturb us, Lord, when
With the abundance of things we possess
We have lost our thirst
For the waters of life;
Having fallen in love with life,
We have ceased to dream of eternity
And in our efforts to build a new earth,
We have allowed our vision
Of the new Heaven to dim.

Disturb us, Lord, to dare more boldly,
To venture on wider seas
Where storms will show your mastery;
Where losing sight of land,
We shall find the stars.
We ask You to push back
The horizons of our hopes;
And to push into the future
In strength, courage, hope, and love.

four

Call of the mermaid

I have two little girls. Actually, they are two big girls now. All grown up, taller than me and they've flown the nest. But having two little girls, means that much of my life has been pink. They loved pink when they were little. And they loved Disney films. Our home was like a shrine to the Disney Corporation and *My Little Pony*.

They would have watched Disney Films on video all day if we had let them. When they got 'into' a particular one, they had to watch it every day for a week. Disney addicts. It was like being slowly brainwashed by Snow White or the snake in *Jungle Book*. To this day, I can recite most of the script of some of those cartoons.

My girls introduced me to *The Little Mermaid*. Wow, that's a hard film to watch without blubbing! As I sat with my girls to watch it, we saw Ariel, the Little Mermaid, singing while in her hidden cavern, which holds all of her treasures, most of which are human objects. The song reveals how Ariel longs to be human and live among their culture, and how she's tired of being a mermaid living under the sea.

To this day, I find this part of the film hard to watch without shedding a tear. You see, Ariel is singing my song. I long to be part of His world – the world Jesus showed me when I was seventeen years old. Ariel's words capture perfectly my longing to live, knowing I'm loved, with Jesus.

Up where they walk, up where they run
Up where they stay all day in the sun
Wanderin' free – wish I could be
Part of that world

When's it my turn?
Wouldn't I love, love to explore that world up above?
Out of the sea
Wish I could be
Part of that world

Ariel was in love with a Prince. She dreamed all day of being with him in his world. It is the tried and tested love story – universally understood all over the world.

When we read the gospels and the Acts of the Apostles, we are really reading an unfolding love story. However, in Ariel's story she is unknown to the Prince - a nobody in his kingdom. In the gospel, it is the Prince, Jesus, who is pursuing the nobodies with his love. *God so loved the world.*

Down on the bottom of the ocean, there were all sorts of rituals and rules that Ariel was required to observe, but she was uninterested in them. She gave up everything to pursue her Prince.

Sometimes, when I'm with religious people, I get depressed. When they start to comment on some group in society or in the world, and speak about them as pariahs - as though God could never love one of *'those'* *people.* There are many Christians who want me to sign things to say I am against something. I don't join in those protests. I don't want my faith to be something negative. I don't want to be known as someone who is just *'against'* a load of stuff. I want to be *for* something. I want the least, the last and the lost to know that, if Jesus welcomed me, he will surely welcome them.

I can get depressed around religious people. But when I read the words of Jesus my heart warms to him. He is different - not religious at all.

Part of our ministry involves working with drug addicts and prostitutes. I remember standing in a car park late one night with my friend Alison, who pioneered this ministry. We were out *'kerb crawling'* and had pulled over to chat to two *'ladies'*. A car drove by and the driver shouted the word 'Slag!' as he passed. One of the girls hurled a tirade of abuse at the driver, punctuated with four-letter expletives. She rejoined our conversation. Occasionally she stepped aside to vomit into a hedge – a side effect of the drug withdrawal symptoms she was experiencing. She was desperate for another 'fix' and so was out looking for 'clients'.

So tell me, what is the most loving thing I can do? Sign a petition condemning prostitution and drug addiction? Or be a friend, like Alison, showing unconditional love, and being there to pray for, and with, these women?

The mermaid in me longs for those girls to be *'part of His world'* – the world of Prince Jesus, where they would encounter love without abuse, and healing for their deepest wounds. But it will only be love and friendship that has a remote chance of touching these wounded Princesses. As the years have passed, both of these women have asked for prayer and encountered Prince Jesus. They may still be stuck, for a while at least, with addictions and chaotic lifestyles, but the love story has begun. Jesus is courting them. And he's a far better boyfriend than their pimps. Though, strangely, Jesus loves the pimps too.

And here's the thing - love cannot be institutional-ised or made into a policy. That is one reason why I dislike the *WWJD? (What Would Jesus Do?)* question. We cannot reduce Jesus down to a set of policies. Read the gospels. What would Jesus do when he meets a blind guy? Well he didn't have a policy on that because it was different every time. He saw the real person and knew them and loved them.

What would Jesus do if he met a prostitute? Again, he doesn't have a policy on that one either. He didn't see a prostitute. He saw a woman made in the image of God and loved her.

What would Jesus do with a Muslim or a Hindu or a gay person or a terrorist or a Jew or a thief or a million-aire or a bus driver or an atheist or a bin man... or me? I don't think he has a standard policy. He is not trite. He loves each one of us. He knows our story. He loves us as we are.

'Won't he change those people?' you may ask. I think when anyone meets the real Jesus they will change. Will that change be what you or I think it should be? Almost certainly not. If you think everyone should change to be like you, get a haircut, take a shower, blow their nose, eat fish on a Friday and vote the way you do, then no, I don't think the change will be what you think it should be. Any change will be the effect of uncon-

ditional love on the broken heart of a man or woman
being restored by Jesus.

'You can safely assume you've created God in
your own image when it turns out that God
hates all the same people you do.'

Anne Lamott

There is something really pure and holy about Jesus.
He doesn't share my prejudices. He is not irritated by
the people who I find irritating. He hangs out with some
very dodgy people. He is not made in my image. That is
what I find attractive about him. He is not of this world.
He is surprising. He is fully himself. He is not trying to
prove anything. He doesn't need defending.

So my first step on this journey into simplicity was
to hold fast to this love story of Jesus – to see his desire
to introduce every man woman and child to his love and
his kingdom - to *seek first his kingdom and his righteousness.*

I set aside any temptation to condemn groups of
people and instead to listen to an individual's story
- to see Christ with them on their journey, even if they
themselves haven't noticed him yet. Jesus gave us a
new command – *Love one another.* I want to tune in to
the individual I am with at any given time. I want, like
the *Na'vi* in the movie *Avatar*, to say *'I see you'*, and
mean it.

The more people I talk to, the more I am convinced
that we are all on a journey groping in the shadows,

trying to take hold of life, looking for meaning and searching for God. And as we do, our Father smiles on us, like a parent smiles when observing the first steps of a child learning to walk.

'And He has made from one blood every nation ... to dwell on all the face of the earth, and has determined their preappointed times and the boundaries of their dwellings, so that they should seek the Lord, in the hope that they might grope for Him and find Him, though He is not far from each one of us; for in Him we live and move and have our being, as also some of your own poets have said, 'For we are also His offspring.'" (Acts 17:26-28)

five

Why did the chicken cross the road?

Not far from where I live in Suffolk is a large field, bordered on two sides by a country lane. In the middle of this field – the size of six football pitches – is a hen house. The inhabitants are *'Free Range'* chickens, meaning they are not caged but allowed to roam free. Most of the chickens stay near the hen house and peck and cluck all day. A few of the chickens wander right to the edge of the field. And a couple wander right out of the field onto the road. Fortunately, the country lane is not busy with traffic. So the ones that peck and explore the tarmac seem safe. These chickens always make me smile. I've often turned the corner into that lane and stopped to let the startled chickens retreat into the field.

A ten-minute walk away from that scene is a row of older chicken houses. Dark sheds. You can smell the chicken poop and hear the clucking. But you'll never see any life there. You won't see the chickens. They are kept locked up in cages, never to see the light of day.

That place does not make me smile. Actually, it makes me a bit sad.

So, why did the chicken cross the road? It's the question that has fascinated mankind down the ages. Why did the chicken cross the road? It is my aim in this book is to reveal why the chicken crossed the road. Many have had a guess as to why this phenomenon happened. Some were humorous. Others less so.

But I can also reveal that this case does not involve only one solitary chicken. There is a whole crowd taking the trip across the road. The question may better be asked, why are all these chickens making the dash through traffic to cross the road? What is drawing them? What's so bad about the side of the road they were on? And perhaps another question needs answering, are any of them planning to go back?

'The future belongs to those who prepare for it today.'

Malcolm X

I was so interested in this movement of poultry that I took a trip. It was a short trip. I just crossed the road. Once you get over there it is obvious why they crossed the road.

Lots of people will say they should never have been allowed to get near the road in the first place, and that the fence should be made more secure for the chickens' own good. But I admire the chickens for going on that journey.

If you're interested, I'd love to walk with you on that journey and explain why the chickens and I crossed the road. The reason may shock, surprise or delight you.

In the discussion about battery farming versus free range farming, passions run high. Those making money from chickens want to keep the battery farming method. It's much easier to control the chickens. Those more concerned with the chickens' welfare may expose the cruelty involved in denying poultry the free-range conditions.

Obviously, my interest is not really in poultry. I've become aware that thousands of people are leaving the church every year. Most of these people are not turning their backs on God. They are living their life and faith outside the church structures. Tired of churches being run like a business or just that it's so dull, trite or disempowering, they continue their journey with God on a lonelier road. This group, sometimes known as *'de-churched'* people, is not small. They vastly outnumber the Christians who go to church. In the UK alone, in 2007, there were two *'de-churched'* Christians for every one church-going Christian.

In 2007, there were two 'de-churched' Christians for every one church-going Christian in the UK.

My purpose in sharing the thoughts in this book is to begin a conversation with a few of these wandering souls. Not to repeat the experience they walked away from in church, but to suggest a better, smaller, simpler way to journey with God.

Billy Graham wrote something in 1965 which with

hindsight now seems to have been prophetic.

'Multitudes of Christians within the church are moving toward the point where they may reject the institution that we call the church. They are beginning to turn to more simplified forms of worship. They are hungry for a personal and vital experience with Jesus Christ. They want a heart-warming personal faith. Unless the church quickly recovers its authoritative Biblical message, we may witness the spectacle of millions of Christians going outside the institutional church to find spiritual food.'

Billy Graham – writing in 1965

And just to clarify, this book is not about starting a house church. It is really about something that many people have never heard of. It's about recovering something of the early church and adapting that to modern life. So please, don't jump to conclusions. I know some readers will want to label this and put it in a box. But the wind blows where it will. You cannot see where it comes from or where it is going. You cannot box the Holy Spirit. So please bear with me.

'Don't be trapped by dogma, which is living with the results of other people's thinking.'

Steve Jobs

six

Artificial additives

I used to really dislike Fridays when I was in the third year of high school. The last two periods before lunch were double 'Games'. The day started normally. We had Maths followed by Science. Then suddenly we got forty minutes of surreal life. We were in a big hall. We had hardly any clothes on. We were hanging from ropes. Mr Blackwell was shouting at us. Other kids were throwing medicine balls at us. It was a jungle. We just tried to survive for forty minutes.

Then we had lunch followed by History and English. There was something just wrong with the flow of that whole day.

Sometimes I find church is a bit like that. You live your life 'normally for six days and then you have *'double church'* on Sunday. For two hours we wear different clothes, someone shouts at us from the pulpit, we're in a big strange building, we all repeat some stuff together, there's people dancing with flags, we hear about a supper but only get a sample of bread and a sip of wine, there is talk of communion with God but we often come out feeling he is further away than before. And then we go home, have a proper meal with a whole slice of bread and a full glass of wine, if we want. We get changed into more relaxed clothes and normality resumes. And just like Fridays with double games, Sundays with *double church* leaves me thinking 'What just happened? Why did we all go a bit weird? Why did we suddenly adopt a different language for two hours? Why did we use phrases we never use the rest of the week? Does God require us to be a bit weird for a couple of hours on a Sunday? Is that what gets us to heaven?'

I know how to decode the weird stuff we do, and I know the history behind it. My point is, the first disciples didn't do that weird stuff. Their meeting, as their life, was seamlessly normal. There was no separation between sacred and secular.

We seem to have added a whole raft of extras to following Jesus. When the good news gets all tangled up with man-made extras, the beautiful can get obscured by the ugly.

When I go looking for Jesus it is quite hard to find the real Jesus. Certain Christians have had such an impact on Christian thought, it is hard not to be influenced by their thinking. But it is only their thinking.

When I look at Jesus, first of all I am seeing Jesus through the eyes of Matthew, Mark, Luke or John. Matthew wants me to know that Jesus was the Jewish Messiah and a King.

Mark wants me to know that Jesus was a humble servant.

Luke wants me to know that Jesus was human.

John wants me to know that Jesus was divine.

Then Peter, Paul and James and others write letters. Then throughout history significant people have influenced how I see Jesus. Clement of Rome, Ignatius, Irenaeus, Origen, Athanasius, St Augustine, Calvin, Luther, D L Moody, Billy Graham, David Watson, the vicar who used to do assemblies at our school, and my friend Brian who introduced me to Jesus. All these people have put a sort of *'spin'* on Jesus and therefore influenced my understanding of him.

We could say that list is 'of God' – a list of benevolent Christians each shedding light on who Jesus is. But what about other influences? What about the Jesus of the white supremacists? What about the Jesus of the pro-slavery Christians who opposed Wilberforce? What about the Jesus of those who slaughtered the Native Americans? What about the Jesus of the *pro-war-with-Muslims* people? What about the Jesus of the Christians in Rwanda in 1994, who taught that to kill a Tutsi is not a sin, it is like killing a snake? Not all these *Jesus-es* are the real Jesus. So is it possible to find the real Jesus? Can I actually meet the real Jesus without being influenced by others?

Thankfully, Jesus is not dead. He is alive today! And as we read scripture and history, from time to time, it seems God has sent his prophets to correct the false image of himself that people had created. At certain times, human followers were so wrapped up in, and passionate about, their religion and the worship stuff, they lost sight of who God really is. Sometimes, it seems, God just tells us to shut up and get real. Our little double-church period may not always be entirely pleasing to God when we neglect the poor and the marginalised.

'I cannot stand your assemblies. Even though

you bring me burnt offerings and grain offerings,
I will not accept them. Though you bring choice
fellowship offerings, I will have no regard for them.
Away with the noise of your songs! I will not listen
to the music of your harps. But let justice roll on like
a river, righteousness like a never-failing stream!'

(Amos 5:21-24)

When we get religious but neglect the least, the last
and the lost, I'm not sure God is too impressed. It was
that very thing that Jesus disliked in the Pharisees. Yet
it is so easy to get all 'spiritual', condemn those who
disagree with us, neglect love, mercy and justice, and
then still feel good about ourselves.

Human beings are very religious. Even the atheists
are religious about their atheism. What human beings
seem to struggle with is grace. It seems too good to
be true. If it is true, it is indeed amazing. The grace
that came through Jesus is so 'not of this world', we
don't know what to do with it. We humans have failed
to resist the temptation to repackage God's grace into
something we are more familiar with.

'When the Greeks got the gospel, they turned
it into a philosophy; when the Romans got it,
they turned it into a government; when the
Europeans got it, they turned it into a culture;
and when the Americans got it, they turned it
into a business.'

Richard Halverson

Grace can be a bit messy. Some years ago I was sitting in our ministry van with a woman who was engaged in prostitution. My friend Alison had jumped out of the van to let the woman get the benefit of the heater in the van. It was a cold night. She was out on the street looking for *'customers'*. She was smoking a cigarette and telling us both a story of how she had stolen things to fund her habit. As a police officer walked past us, she waited until he was out of earshot and then growled a swear word in his direction. She showed me a weeping sore on her shin where she had been injecting heroin. As we chatted, we gave her a prayer card with a message from Jesus on it. As she read it aloud I was quite moved. 'That is beautiful isn't it?' she said. 'I like that.' Then she went off into the cold night to look for a punter to get money for her next fix.

That incident was hardly Morning Prayer or the Eucharist but I sense more grace flowing in those situations than I usually do in a church service. I feel Jesus, the real Jesus, is there on the street. Yet somehow we seem to want to live our lives in a private, gated Christian community and be separate from the world Jesus loves. And, it seems to me, the more we separate ourselves from the world, the more weird and religious we become.

'We are living in an age hopelessly below the New Testament pattern - content with a neat little religion.'

Martyn Lloyd Jones

When we start adding artificial ingredients to the good news, it must seem like a slap in the face to God. Having sent Jesus to repair the relationship and tear the curtain of separation from top to bottom, imagine his sadness when he sees those to whom he extends his grace, sewing up the curtain and adding a load of rules to the grace so freely given. In his book, *The Parables of Grace*, Robert Ferah-Capon, an Episcopal Priest, describes this contrast between our obsession with religion and God's grace freely given.

'The entire human race is profoundly and desperately religious. From the dim beginnings of our history right up to the present day, there is not a man woman or child of us who has ever been immune from the temptation to think that the relationship between God and humanity can be repaired from our side by our efforts.

Whether these efforts involve credal correctness, cultic performances or ethical achievements, or whether they amount to little more than crassly superstitious behaviour, we are all committed in some way to them.

If we are not convinced that God can be conned into being favourable to us by dint of our doctrinal orthodoxy or chicken sacrifices or the gritting of our moral teeth, we still have a hard time shaking the belief that stepping over the sidewalk cracks or hanging our bathroom towels so the labels don't show, will somehow render the ruler of the universe kind hearted, soft headed or both.

But as the epistle to the Hebrews pointed out long

ago, all such behaviour is bunk. The blood of bulls and goats cannot take away sins. Nor can any other religious act do what it sets out to do. Either it is ineffective for it's purpose or the supposed effective intellectual spiritual or moral uprightness it counts on to do the job is simply unavailable.

The point is we haven't got a single card in our hand that can take a single trick against God.

Religion therefore, despite the correctness of its insistence that something needs to be done about our relationship with God, remains unqualified bad news. It traps us in a game where we will always and everywhere lose.

But the gospel of our Lord and Saviour Jesus Christ is precisely good news. It is the announcement in the death and resurrection of Jesus that God has simply called off the game. That he has taken all of the disasters religion was trying to remedy and, without any recourse to religion at all, set them to rights by himself.

How sad then that the church acts as if it is in the religion business rather than the gospel proclaiming business. What a disservice not only to itself but also to a world perpetually sinking in the quagmire of religiosity, when it harps on creed, cult and conduct as the touch stones of salvation. What a perversion of the truth that sets us free; while it takes the news that 'While we were yet sinners, Christ died for us' and turns it into a proclamation of God as one more insufferable book keeper.'

Robert Ferah-Capon - The Parables of Grace.
Needless to say, even if I could get Matthew, Mark,

Luke, John, Paul, Peter, Clement of Rome, Ignatius, Irenaeus, Origen, Athanasius, St Augustine, Calvin, Luther, D L Moody, Billy Graham, David Watson, the vicar who used to do assemblies at our school, to all stand to one side for a moment, I'd still come to Jesus through a bit of *'spin'*. My own culture, prejudices, worldview and preferences also influence how I see Jesus.

What I am seeking is the Jesus *not-of-this-world* – the one who embraced me in 1976. He was so 'other' and different, and, at that moment, no one had yet added any caveats or told me that 'terms and conditions apply.'

The old saying that, 'if we keep doing what we've been doing, we'll keep getting what we've been getting', began to ring true. I started to lose confidence. Not in God or Jesus, but in this institution we call 'church'. Somehow we had narrowed down a world-transforming community to a bland, inflexible institution that we had franchised into every town and city in the land.

seven

Kentucky Fried Church

When I was little, most churches were pretty much the same. Dusty old hymn books with ancient hymns, sung to the accompaniment of an old organ. That was church. There were a few denominational differences but not much.

The local high street was different from today's high street in many ways. It was mostly independent shops with the proprietor living above the shop. I remember when one of the local cinemas closed and then became a 'supermarket' – a really big shop with a butcher, grocer, greengrocer and hardware shop, all under one roof.

Today, when you go down the main street in any large city or town, it will look very familiar. It looks familiar because large companies and multinationals have opened on the high street and put most of the little independent shops out of business. There's usually a *McDonalds* and *Kentucky Fried Chicken* in every high street or town. Diversity and choice have disappeared.

Tesco, Asda and *Morrisons* have taken over. It is like every high street has been copied and pasted from the previous town.

There has been a move to a 'one-size-fits-all' in terms of town planning. This idea, that we can unify outlets for mass consumption, has infected the church. There has been a small move to modernisation in churches, but it resulted in less choice not more. Some have clung on to tradition. Some have gone modern. In these 'outlets' the organ has been replaced by the worship band, the hymnbook replaced by the projector, and the pews replaced by blue- cushioned seating.

Personally, I rarely eat at McDonalds or KFC. I struggle to tell the difference in taste between the food and the packaging. But that's just me. And, for the same reason, I have struggled with the church. The choice is extremely limited. I can have the traditional *finger-lickin'* liturgy, or I can go large at St McDonalds with a *happy-clappy meal*, with extra tithe. If you like either of those two church styles you are very well catered for. You'll find those in every town and village across the UK.

When it comes to what we do in those places, choice is even more limited. There may be very minor differences here and there but you are stuck with a format largely unchanged since the Latin Mass was fixed:

Singing

Announcements

Bible Reading

Sermon

Prayer

Singing

Communion (if included)

Blessing

Give or take one or two very minor tweaks, that is what you'll get. That is the outline for the Latin Mass and not even the Reformation changed that service outline. This format is not in the Bible. There is nothing sacred about it. But that is what the vast majority of churches use every Sunday. This is one sacred cow. The only change the reformation made to this format is that the sermon was given a higher priority, but the outline itself remained largely untouched.

It is not a bad outline. All the ingredients are good. It's just really boring if there is nothing else on the menu.

The *mega-churches* and *wannabe mega-churches* have added drama, flashing lights and video clips, but still with the same basic outline.

To be honest, I am really bored with *St McDonalds happy clappy meal* and the *finger-lickin'* traditional performance at *Kentucky Fried Church*. In fact, pretty much anything led from the front or from a platform leaves me cold. The church began as a community where every person brought something of the *Spirit-in-them,* to share at a gathering. They met in small numbers purposefully so this could happen.

'When you come together, everyone has a hymn, or a word of instruction, a revelation, a tongue or an interpretation. All of these must be done for the strengthening of the church.' (1 Corinthians 14:26)

The modern day Pastor is really the pre-reformation priest – a mediator between God and people. In the church Paul described, there was no manager or professional Christian as the emcee. The Spirit in each person was freely received. The Holy Spirit led the meeting through every member.

By contrast, today's church meetings are a pre-planned performance with a passive audience. And we wonder why people aren't switched on in their faith. We learn mostly by doing not by listening passively. In modern culture we make a distinction between TV '*viewers*' and computer '*users*.' The former is passive. The latter is active.

In the early church, every person had to walk with Jesus in the Spirit and learn directly from him. So naturally their spiritual gifts and fruits developed. Today, people's gifts and fruits are largely stifled or at least controlled by the priest or pastor.

If you are happy with that system, that is fine. If you meet the Lord there, express your spiritual gifts there, and feel empowered in your walk with the Lord, fantastic. For many people the organised church works well. They are happy there. Great. Don't change it if it isn't broken.

For me it is broken. I don't want *Kentucky Fried Church* anymore. I want to recapture something of the early days of the church, when it was a level community of equals, expressing and sharing the Spirit dwelling in each one, with only the Holy Spirit leading the meeting.

Unfortunately, the church does not like deviants and rarely embraces change. The fact that we are in a period of history when great changes are happening is self-evident. The thousands of men and women leaving organised churches every year is another sign of change. Yet many leaders are so wrapped up in the hierarchical system they are resistant to any significant change. For those whose livelihoods depend on keeping the system going, I understand. Change can be difficult.

In Galileo's day, the church so adamantly held to the traditional understanding of an earth-centred universe that anyone presenting evidence to the contrary could be excommunicated. At that time, most Christians believed that the Bible speaks quite clearly about the cosmos. The earth has a foundation (Job 38:4), which does not move (Ps. 93:1; Prov. 8:28). Even the Protestant theologian John Calvin considered geocentricism so fundamentally true that he claimed people who believed in a moving earth were possessed by the devil.

Well times changed. We are not possessed by the devil any more than Calvin was. Centuries of dogma were undone by a telescope. Someone dared to see things from another viewpoint and gradually our understanding of the world changed.

Only as recently as April 1993, did the Pope formally acquit Galileo of heresy, 360 years after his indictment.

'When change is never an option, you have to hope that the world stays exactly as it is so as not to mess with your view of it. I think this explains why some of the preachers on TV look so frantic and angry. For fundamentalists, Christianity sits perpetually on the precipice of doom, one scientific discovery or cultural shift or difficult theological question away from extinction. So fearful of losing their grip on faith, they squeeze the life out of it.

Rachel Held Evans - *Evolving in Monkey Town.*

Clearly the church has changed and evolved over the

centuries. Even in my lifetime, the church has changed significantly. It used to be old ladies who wore hats to church. Now it's the young men, baseball caps askew.

My search for change was made all the more difficult by this *one-bland-brand-fits-all* idea. St McDonalds and Kentucky Fried Church were not an option. But at the time, they were all that was on offer. And then an idea from another world landed in my head.

eight

A thought from another galaxy

After several months of *'godly disturbance'*, I began to feel trapped. Pressure was mounting. I was a Christian, a leader and in full time ministry for goodness sake! I was supposed to 'go to church' somewhere. People had actually started saying things like 'Attendance is really important.' I even began to remember that little cartoon in the booklet *Journey into Life* where the lump of coal fell off the fire. 'Without Christian fellowship our faith will grow cold and die', was the implication. I really didn't want to lose my faith, but *'going to church'* – whatever that means – had become mental and spiritual torture.

One day, I called my friend Martin Garner to chat about something else. After we finished the conversation, I told Martin about my struggle with the whole church thing. I was going on about the difficulty of finding another church. Then, in his usual 'outside-the-box' style, he said, 'Then don't. Don't find another church to attend.' he said.

'But we have to attend church as Christians.' I replied.

'What about another alternative? What about church-less Christianity?' he asked.

'Yeah right!' I said laughing. 'If only that was possible.'

'OK let me qualify that. What about Christianity without the institution we call church?

I'd never been a fan of institutions. And I would be the first to agree that the church is a living organism not an organisation. The question went off in my head like a hand-grenade.

'You're messing with my head now! I'll need to think about that.' I said.

As I put the phone down I had some sort of epiphany. Perhaps even a vision. I saw it clearly. I was on a train. It had pulled into a siding. It slowed to a crawl. Then I saw the end of the line. There were the buffers. The train stopped and I felt that pull of the Holy Spirit saying, 'Get off. This is the end of the line.'

It is hard to explain but something happened that day. I got off the train. As I thought back over thirty years of faith and ministry, I realised I had been on a train. The institution is rather like a train. It runs on tracks and can only go where the tracks go. It speeds along missing the opportunity to take in some of the views. The menu in the buffet car was very limited. But now I was off the train and walking. It was a lot slower but it gives you time to think and take in the view. There is the possibility of going where the tracks don't go and exploring new vistas.

Already I can feel my orthodox friends cringing that I may quickly fall into error unless I am *'in church'*, *'accountable'*, and *'under apostolic leadership'*. (There are three loaded unbiblical phrases right there!) But I'll come back to that later.

I didn't once feel I had 'left the church' – the one that Jesus founded. On the contrary, I felt I was only just discovering it.

As the days past, I seemed to be having a conversation with myself and with God. I'd remember some of the rules I'd held to for a long time and then it seemed God showed me if they were true or false. For example, I continued to feel guilty for a while by not *'going to church'*. I remembered saying to people in the past, 'There's no such thing as a solitary saint. We must come together if we are to grow as Christians.'

But then I discovered Saint Anthony. St Anthony was a solitary saint! He is also one of the biggest influences on present day Christianity. But Anthony began his spiritual journey into monasticism by going into the desert and purposely living alone. Anthony was the first known ascetic going into the wilderness (about AD 270–271), a geographical move that seems to have contributed to his renown. He is notable for being one of the first ascetics to attempt living in the desert proper, completely cut off from civilisation. His lifestyle was remarkably harsher than that of his predecessors. Yet the title of *Father of monasticism* is merited as he was the inspiration for the coming of hundreds of men and women into the depths of the desert, who were then loosely organised into small communities.

What I found fascinating about Anthony was that he was, for a long time, 'a solitary saint' and yet he is held in such high regard by the church. We still tend to prefer dead prophets to living ones it seems. Although Anthony's extended solitude led to the formation of small desert communities, we must not lose sight of that significant period when he was purposely alone. In that season he did not know his solitude would lead to community, he was merely following God's leading.

As these monastic desert communities were formed they developed a culture and lifestyle. There were four notable characteristics:

- *Withdrawal from society*
- *Hesychasm (silence, stillness)*
- *Charity and forgiveness*
- *Recitation of scripture*

Withdrawal from society

The legalisation of Christianity by the Roman Empire in 313AD actually gave Anthony a greater resolve to go out into the desert. Anthony, who was nostalgic for the tradition of martyrdom, saw withdrawal and asceticism as an alternative. When members of the Church began finding ways to work with the Roman state, the Desert Fathers saw that as a compromise between 'the things of God and the things of Caesar.' The monastic communities were essentially an alternate Christian society.

I didn't have any plans to go off and live in the desert but, as someone who is closer to the introvert end of the scale, I prefer solitude and silence. In fact, I require significant blocks of it daily to recharge my emotional batteries. I do like being with people but I struggle with those who stress all the time, and with those whose repressed anger seems to punctuate their speech with feigned outrage.

Hesychasm

Hesychasm (from the Greek for 'stillness, rest, quiet, silence') is a mystical tradition and movement that originated with the Desert Fathers and was central to their practice of prayer. Hesychasm for the Desert Fathers was primarily the practice of 'interior silence and continual prayer.' It didn't become a formal movement of specific practices until the fourteenth century Byzantine meditative prayer techniques, when it was more closely identified with the Prayer of the Heart, or 'Jesus Prayer.'

Hesychast prayer was a meditative practice that was traditionally done in silence and with eyes closed – 'empty of mental pictures' and visual concepts, but with the intense consciousness of God's presence.

As I read about this seeking for inner tranquillity, I realised I had been pursuing that very thing for years but others had labelled it as being antisocial, grumpy or just dull. For me, constant inner stillness had been a passion for decades. The services I attended over the years always seemed too wordy, too organised and even babbling. At last, Anthony gave me permission to be myself.

Charity and forgiveness

The Desert Fathers put a great deal of emphasis on living and practicing the teachings of Christ, much more than theoretical knowledge. Their efforts to live the commandments were not seen as being easy - many of the stories from that time recount the struggle to overcome negative emotions such as anger and judgment of others. Helping a brother monk who was ill or struggling was seen as taking priority over any other consideration.

In my pursuit of seeking first the kingdom of God, I had been passionate for years about how we live out the teachings of Jesus day to day. Anyone can pretend to be holy for two hours on Sunday, but how can we really live in love and forgiveness as a lifestyle. That is what interested me.

Recitation of scripture

The lives of the Desert Fathers that were organised into communities included frequent recitation of the scriptures - during the week they chanted psalms while performing manual labour and during the weekends they held liturgies and group services. The purpose of these practices were explained by John Cassian, a Desert Father, who described the goal of psalmody (the outward recitation of scripture) and asceticism as the ascent to deep mystical prayer and mystical contemplation.

I had been worn out by meaningless liturgy, but the idea of reciting and meditating scripture was something I already did. I would often take a phrase or saying of Jesus and meditate on it during the day while doing daily chores. I held the Bible in high regard and felt that God had spoken to me through Scripture, several times over the years on significant matters.

As I read about the life of St Anthony, Martin's question about living out faith without the institution began to make sense. I felt St Anthony gave me permission to 'get off the train', as it were, to explore spirituality for a season to see if there was more on the menu than *Kentucky Fried Church.*

Changing your thinking is like changing a nappy. You have to take off the old before putting on the new.

'The cave you fear to enter holds the treasure you seek.'

Joseph Campbell

nine

A call to simplicity

So there I was, with my clean sheet of paper. I was going to do church differently, in a non-institutional way. Right. Yes. Well then.

That first Sunday was different. I hadn't been to a church service for months by then but this was the first Sunday I was doing the new thing. Previous Sundays were about *not* doing something – not going to church. But this Sunday was about *doing* something, the start of doing church the new way.

My wife went off to church as usual and I had the house to myself for a couple of hours. Right. This is it. Right. Yes.

I tried focusing on God. Then I prayed for a bit but it was that sort of empty pointless prayer that bounces off the ceiling by virtue of its own insincerity. I know, I'll read the Bible for a bit, I thought. Nothing gripped me. Unusually for me, it felt really boring. I closed the Bible and then a conversation seemed to start. 'Lord, how do I do this new thing? If this is really of you, how do I do it?'

I felt God was slightly bemused by my wanting to *do* something because one thing I'd established was that it was about *being* with him, rather than *doing* something for him. God seems far more focused on just loving us and having us with him in a relationship. We don't expect our children to do anything to earn our love. We love them because they are our children. The whole performance thing – doing something to score religious points, to earn God's love – that is a very religious human idea.

Then I felt God speak in my heart. 'Don, what do you want to do right now?'

The question made me smile. To be honest, as usual I'd like to get this God-slot over with and get back to normal life. 'What I'd really like to do right now, is have a walk into town, buy a Sunday paper and sit outside the coffee shop in the sunshine and read it.'

Then I felt God say, 'Well, why don't you do that then?'

It was strange. I assumed God was saying that class was over for the day, which he wasn't. I felt released to walk into town, buy a paper and have a coffee. The sun was shining and the coffee shop bustling. I got a large coffee and found a table outside in the sunshine. I began to relax and read my paper.

I became distracted. This scene was usually hidden from me. On Sundays I used to always be in church. I didn't really know what the non-church people did. I scanned the customers sitting outside the coffee shop. They were little groups of families and friends, chatting, laughing and eating bacon rolls. And there was another epiphany. The disapproval I'd had of being 'out of fellowship' and the questions of 'where will you get fellowship?' fell away. 'Fellowship' in the Bible (translated from 'koinonia' in Greek) just means friendship, deep friendship. We sometimes use this word 'fellowship' to make a religious rule to put on people – you must be 'in fellowship' to be a valid Christian.

But here were all these people, who I suppose were probably not all Christians, and they were clearly having what the Bible calls fellowship - conversations, questions, laughter, families and friends, all spending time together.

In church we break bread and share wine and call it the Lord's Supper but it isn't really. The sample of bread and single sip of wine hardly constitutes a meal. If I invited you for dinner and gave you that, you'd feel cheated. But Jesus did the whole *'do-this-in-remembrance-of-me'* thing at a proper supper. It was a real meal with his friends, not a religious service. So to actually 'do this in remembrance of' him we should be having a proper meal together.

The idea began to form that what the early disciples did when they met in homes and in the market place, had far more to do with what I saw at the coffee shop that day, than what we did in church services on Sunday.

What if a little group of us could recapture something of the simplicity of the Early Church and meet here and there, as friends and family, and see what the Lord does among us?

The other thing I noticed about the coffee shop was that people would see me there and sometimes come and say hello, or even pull up a chair, get a coffee and have a chat. So that became my Sunday morning for a while, but there was an added ingredient. I wasn't

The Closed Path

I thought that my voyage had come to its end at the last limit of my power, that the path before me was closed, that provisions were exhausted and the time come to take shelter in a silent obscurity.

But I find that thy will knows no end in me. And when old words die out on the tongue, new melodies break forth from the heart; and where the old tracks are lost, new country is revealed with its wonders.

Rabindranath Tagore

having coffee *instead* of church. It *was* church. I was going to the coffee shop with God, open to his leading. Sometimes I marvelled at what unfolded down there. I rarely had idle chitchat. I seemed to start bumping into people who were hurting, or searching, or troubled. God was at work, almost imperceptibly, unnoticed by most people.

I heard a couple of rumours that I had lost my faith, which made me smile because that was the opposite of what happened. My faith was stronger than ever and even finding a new freshness. I hadn't 'left the church' – not the one Jesus started. It came to me that there is actually only one church. Those who ask 'have you left the church?' are really asking 'Have you left our little branch of the church?' which is really neither here nor there. When my daughters come round for dinner, I never think to ask them if they have left the family. They are family and always will be. They both live elsewhere now but they never left the family. If anything, they have enlarged our family.

My foray into a very small spiritual experiment did seem to make some people nervous. Many Christians want everything to stay the same. I suppose I had got off the train. I was going where the rails didn't go and where some people felt I should not be.

'The first Christians argued over whether converts should be required to follow Jewish law. Reformers Wycliffe and Hus were branded as heretics for insisting that people should be able to read the Bible in their own language. When Martin Luther took issue with the church's selling of indulgences, he launched one of the greatest debates of all time about Christian fundamentals, risking excommunication and even death for challenging accepted doctrine. Just a few years later, Protestants themselves systematically executed Anabaptists for holding to the 'heresy' that a confession of faith should precede baptism. And in America, not so long ago, disagreements regarding the biblical view of slavery split denominations. The original Southern Baptist Convention organised, in part, because Baptists in the South did not want to be told by Baptists in the North that owning slaves is wrong. After all, they argued, the Bible clearly teaches that slaves should obey their masters.'

Rachel Held Evans - *Evolving in Monkey Town.*

After a few weeks of listening to podcasts and reading books about a group of people who talked about *'organic church'* I began to see a problem. I lived in a small town and I seemed to be the only person thinking and experimenting with church in this way. As much as I like St Anthony's solitude and withdrawal, I was seeking a new community. But how can we do community if we are the only one who thinks like this in a fifty-mile radius?

One hallmark of this new beginning was that it flowed out of my relationship with Jesus and the Father. That is what being organic means – that growth and change flow naturally from within. They are not imposed or organised from outside, as in an institution or a hierarchy. So I began to have that conversation with God.

'Lord, if there are others in this locality who are on this road, or on a similar journey, please reveal them to me. Let our paths cross and the conversation begin.'

When I prayed that prayer, I really could not see how God could produce like-minded people in my locality. So often when I pray in desperation, I can't see how God could answer the prayer. But that's what convinces me that prayer works – when the answer comes unexpectedly.

'Everything begins with choice.'

The Matrix Reloaded

I had realised by now that there really is nothing sacred about church on a Sunday. The church of the New Testament was not an organisation with an events programme. They didn't 'go to church'. They were a community of people who were the church – the *'ecclesia'* simply meaning 'gathering.' They were church all the time. It was a lifestyle not a meeting, event or organisation. So I became available for God, and to God, all the time. That does not mean I was available to every Tom, Dick or Mary all the time, but I listened to the leading of the Spirit. If I got a 'quiver in the liver', I would make space to meet people.

What unfolded was a series of fascinating conversations. People would text or call me to see if I was free for coffee. I'd meet them at the coffee shop just for coffee. There was no agenda on my part other than friendship. Yet repeatedly a similar conversation would ensue.

Friends would chat for a while and then steer the conversation to troubles they were having with church.

This kept surprising me.

In the past, as a loyal member of the institution, I would try to defend the church while at the same time empathising. But by now, I'd heard such tales, some of which amounted to spiritual abuse, I decided I could no longer defend the indefensible. Sure there are people who will always complain about everything including the church. But there are also some wounded soldiers – wounded by their own side. And then there were people who were just really bored or frustrated with church. I understood that.

So I'd listen for a while, ask a few questions, and then I'd ask the important question. 'Are you enjoying this?'

'What?' people would ask.

'Are you enjoying this – having coffee, chatting about stuff?' I'd say.

'Yes. Obviously otherwise I wouldn't be here.' they'd say.

'Well, what if this was church?' I asked.

'What hold the service in here?'

'No. I mean what if this – you and me drinking coffee and chatting about God and stuff – what if this was church?'

At this point there is always nervous laughter and disbelief.

'Yeh right!'

'No I mean it. What if this is what we did for church?'

'Oooh I don't think that's allowed...'

'By who?'

'But what about....' and so the conversation continued.

And those thoughts always needed a few days to sink in and then people would come back for another coffee and more probing questions.

I think the record was more than three hours and several coffees as we, together, unpacked the grace and love of God through a conversation. People struggling with church, people who'd left the church, people who were struggling to forgive themselves, people who had been physically and spiritually abused - several people began to find healing, restoration and hope for the future. And some just found an inspiring adventure – a new journey with Jesus and his Father.

For me it was a new arena. I'd always felt pressure to share faith one to one. And I had always tackled it like a salesman selling an unwanted vacuum cleaner. I usually failed to 'close the deal'. Put me on a platform in Africa to speak to thousands of people and I could sell the God product. People always responded. But put me on a table in a coffee shop and my sales pitch failed every time, because now my audience could interrupt and ask reasonable questions.

But in this new venture, I wasn't 'selling' a product. I was sharing the ups and downs of my spiritual journey and listening to others do the same. Suddenly I found people who were interested in my journey, as I was in theirs. I wasn't trying to convince anyone of anything I was just being myself. And maybe that was the key. For years I'd tried to be who I thought people in the church wanted me to be. I jumped through hoops for God knows what? Approval? Possibly. To be loyal? Definitely. But my real thoughts I had kept to myself. I could not really put what I thought into words. But now I could.

'Lighthouses don't go running all over an island looking for boats to save; they just stand there shining.'

Anne Lamott

I discovered that we had made the Christian life far too complicated, and far too much about performance and events.

My new little 24/7 church was really simple. We never had to plan events. No buildings were required to be owned or rented. We didn't have to set up a PA system or find musicians. It only required two or more people. It was here and there, now and then. It was simple community. A thought began to form in my mind. For years, like many other ministries, I had pursued 'faster, bigger, more elaborate.' But now I felt a call of the Holy Spirit - a call to *slower, smaller, simpler.* The more I thought about it, the more I came alive. I used to come alive in the pulpit, in churches, speaking at conferences. But now I came alive without an audience – with one other person who was free to interrupt when I spoke. And I was as keen to listen as to speak. If the Holy Spirit was poured out on all flesh, as the Bible says in Acts 2, then I wanted to hear what he was saying through my brother or sister.

It seemed that what I was uncovering was so very different from what everyone assumed was required to do 'valid church', yet it felt so much closer to the early church way than the thing we do on Sunday mornings, with all the scary, sacred cows. More than that, I felt the leading of Jesus almost every day. He was there all the time. I didn't need to wait until Sunday or for an organised event led from a platform. Jesus loved me. And he kept showing up for ones and twos. We never had a programme, so we didn't have to keep cutting him off because we overran the allotted time, like we sometimes do in organised events. It was organic. It carries its own life within.

The church seems to be so locked into a Christian curriculum, a course or some sermon series, that we have lost sight of the fact that God wants a direct relationship with each of us. He himself can lead us. We don't need to be spoon fed by a mediator. God never was a great fan of the mediator thing. That's why he sent his own Son to bring that to an end.

'I myself will tend my sheep and make them lie down, declares the Sovereign Lord.'

Ezekiel 34:15

'But when he, the Spirit of truth, comes, he will guide you into all truth. He will not speak on his own; he will speak only what he hears, and he will tell you what is yet to come.'

John 16:13

ten

Simplicity of belonging

Something in the human spirit engages with life. It
is hard to find a person who doesn't have some sort
of philosophy of life on planet earth. Most of us are
searching for a creed to believe, a song to sing, a flag
to follow. Obviously there are many different religions
and philosophies. But even within Christianity there are
many shades of ideas and opinions. Christians differ on
what they believe about belonging to God's kingdom.

Some Christians think everyone goes to heaven.

Some think most go to heaven but not Hitler and
people like him.

Some think that only a select few get to heaven and
the rest are consigned to some version of hell.

Many Christians carry what they think is a simple,
clear, Biblical view on who is a valid disciple and
acceptable to God. Somehow, perhaps imperceptibly, we have swapped the criteria God uses, for the
criteria the church uses, for who is and isn't a Christian
disciple. It isn't written down but it is often implied in

sermons and conversations. We have invented a gradu-
ating scale of rules, and the more boxes you tick, the
more spiritual you will be considered. It goes something
like this:

Invite Jesus into your heart.

Attend church regularly.

Do the Alpha course.

Read your Bible.

Pray.

Be baptised (and/or confirmed)

Take communion.

Be committed and loyal to the local church.

Give financially.

Tithe.

Submit to the church leadership.

Invite others to church.

Takes notes during the sermon.

*Give some of your time and talents to jobs that need
doing in church.*

Join the church council.

Engage in lay ministry.

Train for full time ministry.

Become a member of the clergy.

If you achieve all of these steps, you will be on the
invisible ladder of 'success' towards being considered
a really spiritual Christian. Quite where the free grace
of Jesus fits into this ladder, I am uncertain. When you
examine these ideas, major flaws are revealed.

Some Christians think that real Christians are those

who have said what is commonly known as *the sinner's prayer.* Christians don't exactly agree on what that prayer is, but basically it is asking Jesus into our heart or life. Over the last thirty years I have led thousands of people in praying this prayer. It is not a bad prayer. Sometimes it doesn't seem to 'take'. No change is detected in the one who prays. They fail to climb the invisible ladder of church success. So we assume they were insincere and therefore the prayer didn't count on that occasion.

The flaw with this idea is that the sinner's prayer only originated in the eighteenth century. It was unknown by most of the world until D L Moody began using it. And then Billy Graham made it widely known in the 1950s.

The other problem is that the sinner's prayer is not found in the Bible. Jesus never told anyone to invite him into their heart or life. Nor did the early disciples.

The prayer is not a bad prayer to pray. It is always good to connect with Jesus. But this prayer, of itself, is not a ticket to heaven, nor a guarantee of a life trans-formed.

If this prayer is the true requirement to enter the kingdom of God, then no one in the New Testament made it, nor did anyone in the first seventeen centuries since Christ. I am still happy to use this prayer as a first step on the road of faith but it evidently cannot be the test of a true follower of Jesus.

Some would say that a real Christian life is revealed in someone by them reading the Bible regularly - feeding on the word, and growing as God's word changes them.

Reading the Bible is not a bad idea. Sixty-six books

revealing the growing revelation of God's relationship with his creation - an unfolding love story. Many times in my life, I have felt God lead me or speak to me in some profound way when reading the Bible.

However, I cannot believe that Bible-reading is a requirement to get to heaven. My Great-grandparents were illiterate. Did God make the requirement to enter his kingdom specifically so it would exclude my ancestors?

More than 796 million people in the world today cannot read or write. Has God made Bible reading a requirement, in order to be acceptable to him when so many, through no fault of their own, would be unable to comply?

Some say that church attendance is a requirement. I sometimes hear Christians say things like *'Every believer should be in church, in fellowship and under apostolic leadership.'*

The flaws with this requirement are many. Firstly, the whole concept of 'going to church' was unheard of until the Conversion of Constantine in 312AD. Before then, the church (in Greek, *'ecclesia'* simply meaning 'gathering'), referred to a community not a building or organisation. As Constantine turned the church into a State controlled hierarchy, the simplicity of that community was lost. It was this move that St Anthony and his followers were providing an alternative to. Unfortunately, most of the Christians complied with the Roman State and became members of this hierarchical organisation.

Constantine largely copied the workings of the pagan temples, which had *temples, priests and rituals.* Thus Christianity lost more of its simplicity and embraced pagan practices, allowing priests to be installed as mediators between God and people. There simply was no church attendance, no hierarchical leader, and no religious buildings for the first 300 years of Christianity.

Even the modern independent church with its Senior Pastor is merely the Roman temple, priesthood and ritual, which Constantine established, in all but name.

I could go on with this list but it may be better to ask another question. How does one know if a young couple are truly in love?

Is it a certain number of dates? Is it that they have sex? Is it that they don't have sex before marriage? Is it how they kiss? Is it how they treat one another? Is it how much makeup she does or doesn't wear?

The problem is, falling in love is not a scientific process. Those involved directly in the relationship could probably tell you if they are in love or not. Outsiders may find it difficult to say for sure.

The problem with making a set of rules for what constitutes a valid conversion to Christ is that it is really about a loving relationship. We have often reduced Jesus teaching about the love of his Father down to three steps to this or four steps to that.

'I recently heard a man, while explaining how a person could convert to Christianity, say the experience was not unlike deciding to sit in a chair. He said that while a person can have faith that a chair will hold him, it is not until he sits in the chair that he has acted on his faith. I wondered as I heard this if the chair was a kind of a symbol for Jesus, and how irritated Jesus might be if a lot of people kept trying to sit on Him. And then I wondered at how

Jesus could say He was a Shepherd and we were sheep, and that the Father in heaven was our Father and we were His children, and that He Himself was a Bridegroom and we were His bride, and that He was a King and we were His subjects, and yet we somehow missed His meaning and thought becoming a Christian was like sitting in a chair.'

Donald Miller - *Searching for God Knows What?*

Sometimes Christians talk as though the process of coming into a relationship with God is in this order: *behaving – believing – belonging.* If you start to live well (*behaving*), and make some sort of commitment of faith (*believing*), that will allow you to join the fellowship (*belonging*).

As I observe real people, and indeed my own coming to Jesus, I see the opposite order of these steps: *belonging – believing – behaving.* Back in 1976 I had a friend called Brian who was a leader at our youth club. Sometimes a few of us went to the pub with Brian. One day he told us about a lady who was healed at his church. I don't think he was trying to convert anyone. He was just amazed that this lady got healed.

About this time, I began reading the New Testament. Something in me was drawing me towards Jesus. Brian arranged for us to visit a children's hospital on Tuesday evenings. During those evenings we learnt important lessons about giving of our time and ourselves to others. Later he connected us with a drug addiction rescue project in Manchester, and we helped them do some fund-raising and chatted to clients.

As I began to think more about God, I hung out with Brian more and more. I attended a couple of retreats at a monastery with Brian. I began to feel I *belonged*. One day I went to Brian's church and had quite a powerful encounter with Jesus. Then I *believed*. I've never fully mastered the *behaving* bit, but Jesus and I are working on that one.

Christians seem to want to make lots of new rules and requirements for people to enter the kingdom of God, when the whole point of the cross and Jesus is that we are not able to save ourselves by our own actions. *While we were yet sinners Christ died for us.*

'The hookers and swindlers enter before us because they know they cannot save themselves, that they cannot make themselves presentable or loveable. They risked everything on Jesus and, knowing they didn't have it all together, were not too proud to accept the handout of amazing grace.'

Brennan Manning - *The Ragamuffin Gospel: Good News for the Bedraggled, Beat-Up, and Burnt Out.*

We need to be really careful about placing terms and conditions at the gate of the kingdom of God. The thief on the cross didn't do Alpha, wasn't baptised and Jesus didn't even lead him in the sinners prayer. He didn't read his Bible. He never went to church, yet Jesus welcomed him (Luke 23:42,43).

We have made the sharing of faith and belonging to Jesus much more legalistic and complicated that Jesus ever did. While the religious people argued about who should get in and who should be kept out, Jesus was welcoming prostitutes, dodgy tax collectors and thieves into the kingdom, without even the sinner's prayer in sight. He made it look like he is trying to get everyone in and we are trying to keep most of them out.

By some people's standards, Jesus was terrible at sharing his faith. He gave sermons with no altar call. He told parables with no explanation. He did miracles and then left town. He never knocked on doors (he said he stood at the door and knocked, but he wasn't being literal about it). He never asked people about where they would go when they died. He didn't ask people to accept him into their hearts. He didn't argue with people who rejected him.

But it wasn't just that Jesus did it differently. Jesus seemed completely ambivalent toward what people thought of him. If they liked him, great. If not, that's their business. By today's standards, Jesus was a rubbish evangelist. Either that, or it is we who have missed the point completely.

I think that belonging to God has far more in common with making and keeping friends, or falling in love, than any *tick box list* to work through. My journey began before I ever met Brian. Jesus began to draw me towards him in my thoughts. I became curious. I read books because I can read. I talked to religious people. I experimented with prayer. I argued with friends. I observed the world around me. That spiritual encounter with Jesus in church that day was certainly significant and central. But the relationship has continued to develop, really, for over five decades.

Looking back I can see that Jesus was involved in my life from birth. Not because of any Christian influences in the family, because I don't think there were any. He was involved because he created me and loved me before I was born. Neither do I think it was just because I was born in a Christian country. I believe Jesus is at work in every life, often unseen, drawing all people to himself (John 12:32).

The human action required to avail oneself of Jesus' love, seems to involve nothing more than some sort of embracing, turning to Jesus or simply accepting it. Perhaps life is a journey for everyone, and the stranger who meets us on the way is Christ, who we can ignore, exclude or embrace.

I love to see people embrace Jesus. I love the gentle transformation he brings to people's lives. But these days, I see the simplicity of that mutual embracing. We can preach it, explain it, recommend it but I am not sure we can package it as some *one-size-fits-all* product. It is a love story, a Prince on a quest, a hobbit discovering his purpose. It is life.

eleven

Simplicity of community

When I became a Christian, I discovered a new community. It was a real organic community. Every member seemed free to express the Holy Spirit who live in them. This organic spiritual community, strangely sat within an organised institution. It was a high, anglo-catholic, Anglican church. The congregation had come into an experience of the Holy Spirit sometime before I arrived. There were events and mid-week home groups, but the life of that community meant that we were in and out of each other's homes even when there was no event on.

Looking back, the real life was in the spiritual community not in the institution. But the two did overlap significantly.

According to Jesus, in John chapter 15, He is the vine, we are the branches and his Father is the gardener. This is a picture of the community of faith Jesus planted. You can see why he told them not to create a hierarchy or institution (Matthew 20:25-28). But that is exactly what humans have done to the community of Jesus over the centuries. Instead of allowing the Father to be the gardener, and let the life of the vine flow from Jesus, equally to everyone, we have been rather obsessed with creating an elaborate trellis-work or hierarchies to shape the vine to our own ideas. Then we wonder why the church is often unfruitful.

In their compelling book, *The Starfish and the Spider,* Ori Brafman and Rod Beckstrom tell the story of Dave Garrision, the CEO of Netcom in 1995 when the internet was hardly known by most people. He was sent to raise funding for Netcom to develop its web services. In one meeting, with potential investors from France, Dave Garrison ran into a problem. One of the potential investors asked, 'Who is the President of the Internet?'

Again and again, Dave tried to explain that the internet is a network of networks with no one in overall control. The idea that anything without a hierarchical structure could function was a foreign concept to these French investors. Everything must have a hierarchical structure or chaos would ensue, according to those gathered.

The book goes onto to contrast the spider-like hierarchy of large organisations – attack the head and the thing dies – and the starfish-like qualities of communities like the internet or Alcoholics Anonymous, which are more organic in structure – there is no 'head or president', so if you kill one part, it just grows back.

I am convinced Jesus planted a 'starfish' organisation – that it is why it survived the brutal persecution of the Roman Empire and every other persecution since. However, since the era of Constantine, the church has been restructured as a 'spider' organisation and is much weaker and ineffective as a result.

It is time to abandon our elaborate trellis structures and allow the Father to be the gardener once again. Let us focus on being fruitful branches organically – with the life flowing naturally from within –like a vine - not imposed top down like a business model.

Most of my subsequent experience with church has been the institution or organisation, without the organic community within. And over the years that can get very spiritually dry.

On several occasions, after I have been chatting to someone about God, Jesus and faith, they seemed interested but have one final stumbling block. 'Do I have to go to church?' they ask nervously. I used to try and make it sound better than it was, but it was this one thing that put people off.

'The church has performed a greater miracle than Jesus:
Jesus turned water into wine. The church has taken the wine of the gospel and turned it into the water of human religion'

Soren Kierkegaard

Frankly, the two hour Sunday service is irrelevant to most people's lives Monday to Friday. This has been one of my problems. 'Invite your friends to the service next Sunday!' the leader would sometimes urge. 'Why would I?' I'd often think. 'If I am bored to tears every week, why would I subject a friend to this?' In the early days, when I had invited friends, I'd often sit cringing as they were treated as targets for the selling of some God product, unrecognisable from anything in the Bible. I'd spend the service rehearsing my apologies to my friend and planning how to rescue the relationship from this disaster.

People are searching for spirituality. Many are seeking God. In some senses the large cathedrals and ancient buildings, when not in use and providing a place of silence, are sometimes places where people sense the divine presence. In our noisy, cluttered, busy world, a place of reflection and silence is helpful to many.

As the church has tried to modernise, it has somehow thought that the rock concert would be a good template for a church gathering. For some this is a breath of fresh air. Personally, I'm not a great fan of rock concerts or large crowds, so the chances of me finding God in such a meeting are very small.

'Many evangelical megachurches, in their hope to create comfortable environments for seekers, have stripped their sanctuaries and worship services of any sense of mystery and the sacred. Their fast moving, high production events may entertain us and their avid employment of modern technology may dazzle us, but many times, they cannot help us hear the still, small voice of God.'

Adam S McHugh - *Introverts in the Church*

Certainly there should be freedom to have all styles of gathering and community. If a rock concert switches you onto God, I think you are well provided for.

The more traditional Christians have explored finding God in expressions of unity. I have had mixed involvement in these gatherings. I used to belong to a ministers fraternal in Manchester where there was genuine respect for each other, value placed on the different traditions and a real friendship between ministers. In other places though, the unity was done because it was felt to be a duty. It was organised by a committee and avoided discussing differences. This form of 'unity' is the kiss of death to community life.

'Eccumemism'

- the belief that gathering corpses will generate life.

Those trying to defend the institutions and organised churches may point to past centuries when the church developed into what it is. They may say it has stood the test of time. They may accuse my little experiment of being unaccountable, under no one's control and a high risk for corruption, error and heresy.

Those accusations just make me think *'Oh Moses, smell the roses!'*

Slice through any portion of church history and you'll find plenty of corruption, error and heresy. Within the institutions and organisations of the church I have witnessed the theft of large amounts of money, sexual abuse, spiritual abuse, paedophilia, violence, greed, hatred, adultery and more. Hardly a glowing track record. The hierarchical structure of modern churches is one way of doing community but it hardly shines out as the best, or even a good, way.

Just because most people do something in a certain way, and have done so for a long time, does not make it the only or best way. Jesus said we would know things by their fruit. The fruit I was experiencing was constant frustration and lifeless ritual. Therefore I wanted to find something that, for me, would bring life, closeness to Jesus, and fresh creativity in the Spirit.

'Whatever brings you down, get rid of it. Because you'll find that when you're free, your true creativity, your true self comes out.'

Tina Turner

Last year I was chatting to a friend who had suffered physical and spiritual abuse in an independent church. Domestic violence was effectively condoned by the church leadership. When the victim sought help she was told it was probably her own fault. This happened decades ago and she eventually escaped both her abusive marriage and the church. The unresolved issues of that experience were still affecting my friend.

As we chatted, I said 'The thing about the Good News is that it is supposed to be good news.' Domestic violence is not good news. The condoning of violence is not good news. Telling the victim to stay in the abusive relationship is not good news. What my friend had encountered was not good news. It was very bad news. Therefore it was not the thing that Jesus gave us.

As we chatted, something seemed to click into place in my friend's thoughts. She had avoided Christians and churches for years, for fear of being hurt again. I was certainly not suggesting she try again. My suggestion was that Jesus is good news. And we can have the good news without joining an organisation or institution. Surprisingly, a few weeks later I heard that my friend was attending a local church, but had found love and support there. She seems to be happy. This is good news - which is available with or without the organisation.

She wrote to me recently about what happened after we talked:

'I am very, very happy. Because of your *'the good news is supposed to be good news'*, I opened my heart again to Jesus. He delivered and healed me emotionally and mentally from all the trauma of those years and I found a great church - a real family. When I walked into the church I felt as though I had put on a dressing gown and slippers and come home. I was wrapped in love and care by God and the church which brought healing and restoration.

That love and care continues and I am truly thankful for you telling me the Good News of Jesus that day. It changed my life.'

This incident teaches me that church isn't something we do at a certain place and a certain time. It is a lifestyle.

'I had never questioned the notion that 'church' was something that happened at a certain location, with certain people, and involved certain activities. I turned this concept upside down and redefined church (for myself) as something that happened everywhere, all the time, with everybody. ...so many things I'd assumed or had been told about God didn't add up.'

Jim Palmer - *Being Jesus in Nashville*

'When the forms of an old culture are dying, the new culture is created by a few people who are not afraid to be insecure.'

Rudolph Bahro

Some people have asked me 'Can two thousand years of church tradition be wrong?' The flaw with that question is that it implies that Jesus built the first cathedral and installed clergy and said 'Do church like that.' The truth is, the church has been constantly evolving since its inception. There are to this day many diverse expressions of Christian community. My problem is that in the UK, some Christians seem to have narrowed that diversity down to an almost one-size-fits-all concept. Clearly that is just not true.

A few weeks of playing at St Anthony, having a season of solitude in the 'desert', and a few people were concerned for my soul. The most common 'correctional quote' was a verse in Hebrews. The first half of the verse was ignored and the second part ripped out of context to 'prove' I was wrong - *'Let us not give up meeting together, as some are in the habit of doing.'* was quoted. In context, the verse is about spurring one another on towards love - the very destination I was aiming for! Added to that, I had not given up meeting together - in fact, rather than meeting for only two hours once a week, I was now meeting with Christians almost everyday, albeit in smaller numbers and in a different location. From my point of view, it is the institution that has given up 'meeting together' because it is obsessed with 'meetings' – things with agendas and chairmen, where 'fellowship' is subordinated to the needs of the institution. And even the services have the agenda of the liturgy – written or unwritten – and the congregation sit passively watching a performance.

In context, I agree and comply with the verse. It is about encouraging one another, not condemning those who do things a bit differently.

'And let us consider how we may spur one

95

'The renewal of the church will come from a new type of monasticism which only has in common with the old an uncompromising allegiance to the Sermon on the Mount. It is high time men and women banded together to do this'

Dietrich Bonhoeffer

another on toward love and good deeds, not giving up meeting together, as some are in the habit of doing, but encouraging one another—and all the more as you see the Day approaching.' (Hebrews 10:24, 25)

I have not stopped meeting together with other believers. I meet together far more – almost daily. And the meeting together is far more meaningful to me because there is no agenda imposed by the institution. There is real fellowship, much deeper than I found before.

There are two things that spur me on to experiment with new forms of Christian community. One is that thousands of people are leaving the organised churches every year. There is a mass exodus. It is the elephant in the room.

According to a survey by Tear Fund, there are huge numbers of what they call 'de-churched' people (those who have a personal relationship with God that have stopped going to Church), such that the ratio of de-churched (33%) to regular attenders (15%) is about 2:1. The survey reports that, through the negative experience of Church, nearly all of these de-churched people are closed to invites to church.

'Christians assemble wherever it is convenient because God is not inclosed in space, but is invisibly present everywhere'

Justin Martyr

The second thing is my own frustration with the status quo. If the bread is stale, what's wrong with baking a new loaf? I understand that if you are managing an organisation you need members, to provide the finance through the offering, to keep the system going. I have no doubt the organised and traditional churches will keep going in the present form or something like it. It is just that I can see a much simpler way.

I believe the basics for Christian community are very, very simple. When Jesus was asked about how to please God he told his questioner what we call the *Great Commandments* – love God and love others.

When he was departing, he gave his disciples what we call the *Great Commission* – make disciples.

So as far as I can see, Jesus' pattern for the new community is very simple:

Love God

Love others

Make disciples

The institution or organised church has added to that list at least four more things. A building, events or services, paid clergy or leaders, and, as these extras cost money, a budget.

So the organised church list of basics is:

Love God

Love others

Make disciples

A building

Services /events

Clergy / Pastor

A budget

As the church has developed in modern times, all sorts of things have been added. Currently the list probably looks something like this:

Love God

Love others

Make disciples

A building

Services /events

Clergy / Pastor

A budget

A worship band

Lighting

P A system

Projector

Screen

Laptop

Tithing

Children's workers and facilities

etc...

The longer the list gets, the more likely it is that the first three items – the only ones Jesus mentioned – become lost in the work of keep the system going.

As I began to embrace the simplicity of community, I not only found it far more peaceful and liberating, but it allowed me far more time to focus on loving God, loving others, and sharing the beauty of that in a natural way.

I suspect some folks think I have just dropped out for a season and am having a rest. Less charitable people may say I am being lazy. Well God bless them.

The truth is, a little community of simplicity is forming and there are many of these across the world. It makes some Christians nervous but I have to say, once I got over my feelings of insecurity, it became a beautiful thing.

I still engage with organised church because, from time to time, I am invited to speak at such meetings. And that is fine. What surprises me each time, is how much I had forgotten about the passive audience thing. I have even started telling people to interrupt me when I am preaching or teaching. We grow by functioning, not by passively watching and listening. Jesus calls us to engage with the kingdom of God, not attend a worship concert and sit passively, letting it wash over us. Sometimes we do find it helpful to be a passive receiver, especially when we are tired or have been under stress. I understand that. I just don't think it should be the norm.

The more I reflect on simple community, the more I keep coming back to St Anthony. The monastic communities tend to embrace simplicity. As I searched for a simple community, the idea of a new sort of monasticism emerged. Not a monasticism where we buy a large country house and all live together, but rather one where we remain where we are – integrated into society but perhaps hold a common bond of intention - an intention to live our spiritual life simply, thus freeing us all up to be far more generous to the poor and to each other.

So what does this *Free Range* discipleship look like? I hesitate to answer that question because, for me, the

fundamental basis to it is being led by the Holy Spirit -
to try and walk in that lifestyle, that Jesus spoke about,
when he said he only did what he saw the Father doing
(John 5:19). If you are thinking of going down this
route, my key advice would be - do not start some new
group or work. It is not about organisation but about
relationship. Work on listening to the Spirit and to your
own heart. Silence the clamouring voices that urge
you to start an organisation because that will quickly
become identical to, and as frustrating as, the organisation you left.

Live knowing you are loved because of *who you are*
not *what you do.* Let growth come from within like in
nature, slowly, simply, beautifully.

My journey into simplicity is sometimes caricatured
as '*He just sits in coffee shops.*' It isn't that at all. That
would be like saying Jesus was '*just a bloke who told
stories*'.

Day to day, for me, it is investing time in relationships, particularly with those on a similar but not
always identical journey.

It is listening to the Spirit, in those around us, in
creation and in the scriptures.

It is experimental.

It values daily solitude and daily connection with
others.

It holds a constant awareness of Jesus and his Spirit.

It shies away from angry situations yet confronts
injustice.

It puts family first.

It rarely organises events.

It pursues inner quietness at all times.

It shuns complexity and being over organised.

It embraces simplicity in all things.

It values smallness.

It loves the poor.

It embraces the least, the last and the lost.

It makes space for contemplation.

It is a conversation not a monologue.

It is not selling anything.

It is not buying anything.

It has its faults yet embraces them.

It seeks out laughter, love and life.

It asks questions without expecting neat answers.

It is not competitive.

I have a few friends who would call themselves 'Free Range'. But each of us is living it out a slightly different way. And that is OK. Each respects the other. We journey together through life. Just as free range hens are not caged in, free range disciples are free to roam, to think, to explore and, most importantly, to ask questions.

The meal and the conversation are paramount. To be together and aware of the Father's love for us is key. And yet so is solitude and personal space.

'Dynamic and erratic, spontaneous and radical, audacious and immature, committed if not altogether coherent. Ecumenically open and often experimental, visible here and there, now and then but unsettled institutionally. Almost monastic in nature but most of all enacting a fearful hope for society.'

William Stringfellow - 'An ethic for Christians and Other Aliens in a Strange Land'.

'To be right with God has often meant to be in trouble with men.'

A.W. Tozer

twelve

Simplicity of leadership

'These things I have written to you concerning those who try to deceive you. But the anointing which you have received from Him abides in you, and you do not need that anyone teach you; but as the same anointing teaches you concerning all things, and is true, and is not a lie, and just as it has taught you, you will abide in Him.' (I John 2:26, 27)

Shortly after the Church of England changed its rules to allow women into the priesthood, I was speaking at the Anglo Catholic Charismatic Convention, at Ditchingham in Norfolk. During one of the coffee breaks, my old friend Father Dennis Nichols began chatting to me. Dennis had retired by then and was a lovely old priest. The sort that would make you want to become Anglo-catholic. He had a cheeky smile and was full of grace, a very gentle man.

Dennis, like most people at the convention, had decided to align themselves with the Forward In Faith movement, rejecting women in the priesthood. It was the hot topic of the day. Perhaps my evangelical Bible teaching at the Catholic conference had made Dennis curious as to where I stood on the issue.

'Do you believe in the ordination of women?' Dennis eventually asked me with a smile.

'Dennis, I don't even believe in the ordination of men!' I replied.

He looked over his glasses at me.

'Surely you accept my ordination?' he asked.

'It depends what you mean by 'ordination'.' I said.

'Well you believe in the priesthood of all believers, don't you?'

'Yes. I think that is the priesthood I believe in.' I said.

Dennis smiled his gentle smile as the bell went to call us to the next session.

My ministry over three decades has taken me through all shades and style of the church. At the end of the convention, we shared in a concelebrated mass with three priests leading the service, bells and smells, a few Hail Marys, and the communion wafer placed in a monstrance and adored for a period of silence.

The following Sunday I was speaking in a former Brethren Chapel, where things were very low key by comparison.

I never found this constantly shifting service shape a problem. In fact it taught me that there are thousands of expressions of worship and faith in Jesus. What did strike me though, was the passion with which each group held to their way of doing things.

And in each situation, there seemed to be a separation between the leaders and the people. Father Dennis and I had touched upon it during that coffee break. Even saying that I believed in the priesthood of all believers (1 Peter 2:9), I wouldn't at that time, have known what that really looked like. Perhaps my ex-Brethren friends were the closest example, but I think even they had 'Elders' who were allowed to do some things that ordinary members were not.

As I looked back through history, it is clear that the separation between clergy and laity was established under Constantine's influence, largely borrowed from the pagan temple worship of his day. He superimposed the 'temple, priest and ritual' pattern of the pagans, on to the church of Jesus.

'The clerical system of church management is exceedingly popular, but the whole thought is foreign to Scripture.'

Watchman Nee

The proliferation of the independent churches in our day, initially seemed to abandon the 'temple, priest, ritual' idea of Constantine. But on further examination, it is identical but renamed. House of God, Pastor, Praise service are really Temple, Priest and Ritual by another name.

And the demands of the independent churches are

virtually identical to the hierarchical priesthood of Rome.

Basically, the subliminal and, at times, overt message of the independent churches is that everyone needs to be in church, with an apostolic leader telling everyone what to do. The Pope could not wish for more. Unfortunately, that system has produced virtually no fruit at all in church history.

'Who is your covering?' 'Who are you accountable to?' These are the questions the hierarchy will always ask. Those concerned with the hierarchy of the Pharisees even asked Jesus this question.

'Jesus entered the temple courts, and, while he was teaching, the chief priests and the elders of the people came to him. 'By what authority are you doing these things?' they asked. 'And who gave you this authority?'' (Matthew 21:23)

Jesus refuses to answer them. They viewed him as a dangerous heretic, pretty much as today's church hierarchy views anyone unwilling to answer that question as a heretic. The clergy / laity idea is so engrained that most people assume it is biblical to be accountable to a human leader in the church. However, the Bible nowhere teaches that accountability was ever delegated to men or women. We are all accountable to God directly.

'But I say to you that for every idle word men may speak, they will give account of it in the day of judgment.' (Matthew 12:36)

'So then each of us shall give account of himself to God.' (Romans 14:12)

'Therefore judge nothing before the time, until

the Lord comes, who will both bring to light the hidden things of darkness and reveal the counsels of the hearts. Then each one's praise will come from God.' (1 Corinthians 4:5)

'And there is no creature hidden from His sight, but all things are naked and open to the eyes of Him to whom we must give account.' (Hebrews 4:13)

There is a form of accountability in the New Testament, but it's not part of the pyramid world system. Biblical accountability is mutual accountability – it is part of the 'one another' system. In this system we are accountable to one another on an equal footing. We are to love 'one another', care for 'one another', confess to 'one another', pray for 'one another'. It's the kind of organic mutual deference we see in the Trinity.

'To put it another way, according to the New Testament, there is no clergy/laity distinction. Instead, all Christians are *kleros* (clergy) and all Christians are *laos* (laity).

The clergy/laity dichotomy is a tragic fault line that runs throughout the history of Christendom. Yet despite the fact that multitudes have taken the low road of dogmatism to defend it, this dichotomy is without biblical warrant.

The word 'laity' is derived from the Greek word *laos*. It simply means 'the people.' *Laos* includes all Christians—including elders.

The word appears three times in 1 Peter 2:9–10, where Peter refers to 'the people [*laos*] of God.' Never in the New Testament does it refer to only a portion of the assembly. It didn't take on this meaning until the third century.

The term '*clergy*' finds its roots in the Greek word *kleros*. It means 'a lot or an inheritance.' The word is used in 1 Peter 5:3, where Peter instructs the elders against being 'lords over God's heritage [*kleros*]' (kjv).

Significantly, *kleros* is never used to refer to church 'leaders.' Like *laos*, it refers to God's people—for they are His heritage. According to the New Testament, then, all Christians are 'clergy' (*kleros*) and all are 'laity' (*laos*). We are the Lord's heritage and the Lord's people.

To frame it differently, the New Testament doesn't dispose of clergy. It makes all believers clergy.'

Frank Viola - *Beyond Evangelical Blog*

We do not find Jesus giving the apostles a certificate, a licence, or special clothing or titles. He breathed on them and gave them his Spirit. Never once did Jesus suggest a two-tier system for church life. Some people will always be leaders because that is their anointing, personality or gifting. But in the church of Jesus there is no executive role for humans. He reserved that role for himself.

The term 'laity' is one of the worst in the vocabulary of religion and ought to be banished from the Christian conversation.

Karl Barth

One of the temptations for Christians is to read into the scriptures their own culture and traditions. But we would do better to allow the Bible to challenge our culture and traditions, if we are to touch the hem of Jesus' robe. There were clearly Jewish hierarchical systems in use in Jesus' day. Their nation was occupied by Rome. That was one monolithic hierarchy. Everyone knew their place. The Roman Centurion who came to Jesus for the healing of his servant, even expressed his faith in terms of Roman hierarchy.

Yet when Jesus began to establish the new community of followers, he expressly commanded them never to use that model in the kingdom of God. He was growing organic communities not building an organisation.

'Jesus called them together and said, "You know that the rulers of the Gentiles lord it over them, and their high officials exercise authority over them. Not so with you. Instead, whoever wants to become great among you must be your servant, and whoever wants to be first must be your slave - just as the Son of Man did not come to be served, but to serve, and to give his life as a ransom for many."' (Matthew 20:25-28)

So just to clarify, I am not against leadership in the church. I just believe we should all be leaders. In organic communities people lead in the moment, in their anointing. A prophet may be the leader for the few moments he or she is prophesying. Then maybe someone with the gift of teaching shares an idea and leads for a moment. And so on.

Some years ago, I was in Nigeria with my friend Andy Economides. At an evening service, where about 5,000 people had gathered, Andy preached the message of the good news. Many people responded to his message indicating that they wanted Jesus in their life. After the response, the plan was to lay hands on the sick and pray for healing. For whatever reason, Andy, who is very capable and familiar with healing ministry, called me to the platform and asked me to lead that healing ministry. That ministry is easy for me to do because I have that anointing. Andy did not appoint me to any office in the church, nor declare me bishop of the healing ministry. He simply asked me to lead that part of the meeting. Organic leadership is a bit like that.

The ministry gifts listed in the Bible (Ephesians 4:11) are not offices in the church, but anointings for certain situations, or a role a person may excel in. Any believer should be able to lead in some of those areas from time to time as the Holy Spirit leads. And he will lead, if only he can get our man made hierarchies to move over for a few minutes.

The Holy Spirit was poured out on all flesh - men, women, old and young. My heart longs for each Christian to lead for a moment in an atmosphere of mutual deference to each other, and by the Holy Spirit's leading.

Today, the favourite way to exalt leaders above everyone else is to call them 'Pastor.' The word 'pastor' is only mentioned once in the New Testament, and even then not as an office in the church. In fact, it is only mentioned in plural – 'pastors' – not 'pastor' – meaning a few people in the gathering who care for others naturally. Not a manager of a local group. How it became hijacked as a replacement for the word 'priest' is beyond me. And as for the phrase '*Senior Pastor*' - where the heck does that come from? Not from the Bible that is for sure.

Do I therefore reject all leaders? No. The doctrine of the priesthood of all believers means that the Pope is sometimes right. I long for all of us to lead, here and there, now and then, by the Holy Spirit inside us. What I find unhelpful is people having titles and status, as though only professional Christians, and certain holy men and women, can be used by God to express his love in the earth. Jesus said we should not lord it over others as in the Roman hierarchy. This we have summarily failed to obey. Rather than shunning the hierarchy Jesus told us to avoid, we have embraced it, affirmed it, enjoyed it and used it to take control over others.

Out in Africa I have sometimes been introduced to leaders and been told they are *Archbishop, Apostle, Worldwide President* of some ministry I have never heard of. This is no longer restricted to Africa. Titles in the UK and the USA are getting just as long these days.

So what is simple leadership? The first thing to say is that lots of my friends who are called 'Pastor', 'Rev', or 'Father' or whatever are actually doing something like simple leadership but within the structure and restrictions of organised church. All strength to them. They are gentle people who have no interest whatsoever in controlling, bullying or intimidating others. They are natural leaders and just want to make a difference. And they are. The danger is when the wrong people get into those positions of power.

So, simple leadership - what could it look like? As we get to know each other, as we live and work together, we can recognise the strengths and weakness in each other. As we minister life we defer to the gifts in each other. Often when the subject of healing comes up, people sometimes defer to me because I've written books about healing and seen some amazing miracles. I don't demand or expect people to defer to me, but if they do, I am happy to lead in that area. I have nothing to prove and am equally as happy for others to lead in that area. When they do, I am attentive because I expect I'll learn something. We lead each other like a tag team when we have nothing to prove.

Until you step out of the hierarchy, you will struggle to relax into any sort of simplicity of leadership. You'll always feel you have something to prove, because you'll always feel you could be further up in the hierarchy.

In simple organic leadership, none of that stuff matters. Leadership becomes a gracious dance we can all engage in, and we can relax as we dance.

thirteen

Simplicity of the word

When I was a teenager, living at home with my parents, occasionally someone would knock at the door. There were seven people living in our house, so whoever was available answered the door. One day there was a knock at the door and I was nearest. I opened the door and a young lady and her friend were standing at the door. They were friendly and started talking about God and the Bible. 'Oh no!' I thought, 'It's religious people!' My mind went into overdrive. How could I extract myself politely from this conversation? I remembered something a friend of mine had said when he was confronted with religious people. I thought this would do.

'Oh you can't believe the Bible.' I said, with full confidence. 'It is full of contradictions.'

'Really?' said the lady. 'Show me one.' she said handing me her Bible.

Embarrassed, because I had never read more than the first three chapters of Genesis, I handed her Bible back and said I was too busy at the moment.

I then realised that to win that argument, you had to know where the actual contradictions were. I didn't think about it too much that day, but I made a mental note to try and read the Bible and see if I could spot the contradictions.

A few years later, as I got older, I began to be curious as to why we were here on earth and what life was really about. When I was out in Manchester City Centre, instead of avoiding religious people handing out leaflets, I would chat to them, take their literature and read it on the bus on the way home.

I bought a couple of books on spirituality but they seemed a bit weird. Later on, as I mentioned earlier in the book, I met Brian, a telephone engineer who went to church and had several conversations about God and spirituality. Brian used to go on retreat to a monastery in Yorkshire some weekends, and invited me to join him. I wasn't sure what I was doing but I was fascinated to meet the monks and read some of the books in the library.

The monastery had a little bookshop and I found a copy of the J B Phillips translation of the New Testament in plain English. This was helpful on two points. Firstly it was in plain English – no 'thee' and 'thou' and 'Verily, verily.' Secondly, it was only the New Testament, which meant I didn't get bogged down by the sprawling history of Israel before reading about Jesus.

I did not discuss this purchase with anybody. I began to read the gospels as one would read a novel.

I worked at a factory near Oldham in those days, and read the gospels in my lunch hour. I was sometimes mocked by friends who said I'd 'got religion!' But I hadn't. I was just gripped by the story of Jesus.

By the time I got to the end of John's gospel, it was as though I'd had a close but not direct encounter with the Jesus in the story. I pondered at how this story had come to be written. Who was the author? Did they make up the story? And if they did, what colossal incident in their life had given them such an inspirational storyline?

Looking back, I am sure this plain reading of the gospels softened my heart towards Jesus. A few months later, when I had the encounter in church where I felt I met Jesus, it seemed that the man in the story was alive today and in touch with me in some strange and wonderful way.

As I continued on my spiritual journey I came to value the Bible. I bought several and kept one with me when I went to church. I underlined and highlighted it during sermons and talks I listened to.

A friend at the church introduced me to the preaching of Billy Graham on *Radio Luxembourg*. I was impressed with Billy Graham's preaching style. The authoritative way he would punctuate his sermons with the phrase '*The Bible says...!*' and then give a proof text for his point. This style fascinated me and, perhaps, I thought we could prove God to the world if only we grasped enough proof texts. I became obsessed with noting down certain Bible verses and reading books that had a lot of proof texts.

Years later when I was in full time ministry, I ordered one of the first computer Bibles. The entire Bible on a computer! Now, if I had a vague idea of an obscure text I could rip out of context, to prove my point, I could search for it and find the exact wording and Bible reference. To my new-found legalism, this was gold.

From time to time, I became aware in arguments that my tendency was to lob a proof text in like a grenade in order to end all discussion. I also observed that doesn't always make you popular.

As I look back now I am slightly embarrassed by all of that. I had discovered something in a book that initially came to me like a love story or even a love letter. Within a couple of years, I had started using it like a legal document, or a constitution or like a lawyer referring to a previous case to prove his point of law. The love of the love letter had been trampled underfoot because I didn't want anyone to question God or disagree with his word.

Quite how I missed it I am not sure. The Pharisees came to Jesus using the Old Testament as a point of law and he blew them out of the water every time. He also went around saying things like *'You have heard it said... but I say...'* and then seemed to contradict or expand the Old Testament. If you were a person like me, in Jesus day, who knew what the Bible said, and Jesus kept changing it, I think you would pretty frustrated.

Then I also observed that, if having a legal document that ended all discussion was what God wanted, why didn't Jesus just write one? He didn't write a book. Of all the people who could possibly be qualified to write a legal document for God, Jesus was number one! But he didn't do it.

'Writing in scrolls, however, was not something that interested Jesus. He never sat down and wrote a mission statement. Instead, He accumulated friends and allowed them to write about Him, talk about Him, testify about Him. Each of the Gospels reveals a Christ who ate with people, attended parties, drank with people, prayed with people, traveled with people, and worked with people. I can't imagine He would do this unless He actually liked people and cared about them.'

Donald Miller - *Searching for God Knows What?*

Throughout church history people have argued theological points and used the Bible to prove their arguments. And it is not a bad idea to talk, and think and argue and discuss. But we have to recognise that we Christians used to burn and behead each other for the crime of disagreeing.

The church used to believe in slavery and *proved* it from the Bible. No one is queuing up to make that argument anymore. And those who brought about the abolition of slavery also *proved* slavery was wrong by arguing from the Bible.

Of course, the simplicity of the Early Church was enhanced by the fact they didn't have the Bible. They had the Old Testament and a living relationship with Jesus through the Holy Spirit. But they were not walking round with a leather-bound Old Testament under their arm, with highlighted verses.

Paul was prolific in dictating letters and scrolls across the rapidly spreading Early Church. As he dictated them, I am not sure he thought he was writing anything that would be used as a legal constitution later on, but rather something to be passed around believers to weigh the wisdom he communicated.

Justin Martyr, in the early 2nd century, mentions the *'memoirs of the Apostles'*, which we now know as the Gospels.

The first council that accepted the present Catholic

canon (the Canon of Trent) may have been the Synod of Hippo Regius in North Africa (393). The acts of this council, however, are lost. A brief summary of the acts was read at and accepted by the Councils of Carthage in 397 and 419. These councils were under the authority of St. Augustine, who regarded the canon as already closed.

So for nearly 400 years, what we quote as *'the word of God'* to prove our religious points, was not settled or agreed. And even when the canon of scripture became settled, some Christians advised believers to keep an open mind in case we misread scriptures and find ourselves stuck in a theological dead end.

'In matters that are so obscure and far beyond our vision, we find in Holy Scripture passages which can be interpreted in very different ways without prejudice to the faith we have received. In such cases, we should not rush headlong and so firmly take our stand on one side that, if further progress in the search for truth justly undermines this position, we too fall with it.'

St Augustine - *The Literal Meaning of Genesis.*

In today's modern, global, multi-cultural world, people of several faiths quote their holy books before committing terrible acts. Christian America invaded Iraq with the seeming support of Republican Christians.

The command of Jesus to 'love your enemies' seems to have been lost somewhere down the line.

In 2005 there was even a presenter on a Christian TV show who infamously suggested that the government of America should assassinate Venezuelan President Hugo Chavez to stop his country from becoming 'a launching pad for communist infiltration and Muslim extremism.'

Islamic terrorists quote the Koran. And in both cases, I am sure peaceful Christians and Muslims respectively cringe with embarrassment.

I view myself today as a recovering Pharisee. I used to judge many people while God loved them. I forgot how much grace and freedom he gave me. I condemned those who were different from me, in my thoughts and my speech.

St Paul, who would have been well able to win most arguments using the Bible as a legal document, tells us that we can know God by simply observing nature, without any recourse to a holy book.

'For since the creation of the world His invisible attributes are clearly seen, being understood by the things that are made, even His eternal power and Godhead, ...' (Romans 1:20).

This may explain why the parables of Jesus featured the simple things of nature like sowing, reaping, fishing, doors, pearls and sheep. Paul also tells the disciples at Corinth that they themselves are living letters of good news.

'You are our epistle written in our hearts, known and read by all men; clearly you are an epistle of Christ, ministered by us, written not with ink but by the Spirit of the living God, not on tablets of stone but on tablets of flesh, that is, of the heart.'

(2 Corinthians 3:2-3)

Our lives – how we live and do relationships - will tell and prove more than any legal debate will. People don't care what you know until they know that you care.

As I rise to the challenge of God to find simplicity in all things, when it comes to the word, I remember my factory days. When the unfolding love story melted my heart. When my weary soul found a grace so wide and deep. God didn't reveal himself in a legal document. He revealed himself in a storybook. His son's parables, far from ending all discussion, provoke questions, thoughts and more discussion. And in that love story, I read that even if there was a court case against me, all charges have been dropped.

I am trying, in my search for simplicity, not to be a Pharisee anymore. I don't want to prove you wrong or me right by stinging you with a verse of the Bible. I've no interest in those sorts of discussions anymore. If we are not going to listen to each other, but formulate our answer before the other person has even finished talking, what is the point?

These days, I'm more interested in hearing the story of your journey, and sharing some of mine - to get a little wisdom from you for my journey.

There are lots of parts of the Bible I don't really understand, even after all these years. Sixty-six books written by different people over thousands of years. And yet, in 1976, at my workbench in the factory near Oldham, I read a story that drew me with chords of love. It is a simple story and yet so profound the world still talks about it all these thousands of years later. Here and there, now and then, I hear the whisper of the Father through that book. And it still has the power to melt my heart, change my thoughts and cause me to pursue miracles.

When that lady knocked on our door and handed me her Bible all those years ago, I think she may have wanted a legal argument to prove me into some religion. Or maybe she had discovered the love story in the book and just wanted to share it. I'll never know. If she came to use it as a legal document, I am glad my ignorance saved me from that conversation.

If she came that day, because she had discovered the love story, I may have missed an opportunity to learn something. Because the real thing – the love story thing – it really is good news.

If I have a text I am still proving things from, it would be Acts chapter 29. And before you waste time looking it up, I'll let you know, it isn't there in the Bible. Luke stops his writing at Acts chapter 28. Acts is the story of the new community of Jesus' followers. That story is still being written today. Not by Luke, but by men and women who have embraced the simplicity and love of the word, and more importantly its author.

fourteen

Simplicity of the meal

My friend Hil asked me to join him on a road trip to Grenoble in France. He needed to collect his daughter's belongings as she was moving back to the UK. His daughter was flying back home but before that, we needed to get there and clear her flat.

Suffolk to Grenoble and back is a round-trip of 1,400 miles, which we planned to do over three days. We have quite different personalities – I like to know in advance what will happen. Hil enjoys spontaneity a whole lot more than I do. I like some spontaneity but only if it is personally planned beforehand by me. In our favour we both like France – its culture, rolling countryside and the vin rouge.

I'd been to France four times before and on three of those occasions it was closed. If you have ever been to France, you'll know what I mean. On public holidays everything is closed everywhere.

We left the Suffolk shortly after 4 am to catch a 9:30am ferry crossing. We arrived in Dunkirk and Hil navigated as I drove South towards Dijon, our target destination for the first night. At the time, we were both thinking through the idea of being *Free Range* in our Christian walk, and we chatted about this and many other things as we drove.

We tried to get some lunch but everywhere was closed except a motorway service station where the sandwiches were grim. We ate a few bites and binned the rest. We pressed onto Dijon. On our arrival at the hotel, we found the restaurant was closed. We drove back into the centre of Dijon and found most places were closed there also. We found a little convenience store and bought a baguette, some ham and a bottle of vin rouge. We took these back to our room. Exhausted from 15 hours of travelling, we consumed the ham, bread and wine before falling asleep.

The next day, we arrived in Grenoble and found Hil's daughter. We had lunch in Grenoble and had a walk round, seeing a few of the sights. Late afternoon we went and bought a few things to eat at the flat where we were staying, like the previous night.

On the third day, we packed all Ella's belongings into the car and said farewell. After a long day of driving we reached Laon in Nothern France and stayed at a hotel there for the night ready for the early drive next morning to catch the ferry.

As we settled down for the night we were eating a baguette and enjoying some red wine.

'Did you notice,' said Hil, 'that we have shared communion everyday on this trip?'

'What do you mean?' I asked

'Every evening we have broken bread and drank wine together.'

Hil's simple but profound observation got me pondering. As I had been thinking about simplicity of gathering together, the one thing I hadn't resolved was what communion would look like in the simplified Free Range way. Maybe Hil was onto something. It had been so natural to share bread and wine on this trip, and something told me that what Jesus did at the Last Supper was not a religious act, but something very natural, to which he attached a new meaning. Surely breaking of bread should be more like having friends round for dinner than some religious ritual.

Hil's comments made me wonder about the simplicity of breaking bread and what that would look like. But somehow there seemed to be a piece of the jigsaw missing.

Then my friend Martin Garner called. He had just returned from Israel where he had been working as a guide at the *Hula Valley Bird Festival.* The Hula Valley in Northern Israel is one of the most important stopover and wintering sites for southbound migrant birds through the Great Rift Valley. It is here that complete populations of birds stop to 'refuel' before reaching the desert strip to the south.

The region serves as a migration flyway for thousands of Common Cranes, White Pelicans, Ducks, Waders and Passerines every year. Over 300 species are seen there annually including some of the rarest European birds of prey.

Martin had a great time and shared some of his stories. But one incident had amazed him. After finishing for the day, he was travelling back to his hotel with his host. His friend asked what he was doing for the evening and wondered if Martin wanted to join his family for dinner. He told Martin it would be a bit 'Jewish', obviously, but if he was OK with that, he was welcome. Martin agreed to join his friend.

The meal was a simple family meal that began with singing a Jewish prayer – it was a *Shabbat* meal as the family began their Sabbath. What amazed Martin was that after the prayers, his host broke bread and shared some wine around the table. For this family, it was just the usual family dinner, with the children sitting around the table. What struck Martin was that he appeared to have stumbled upon something so close to the Last Supper. Surely this had been how Jesus and the disciples had shared that meal. Informal, a few Jewish prayers, bread broken and shared, wine poured out. It was what Jewish friends and families did to begin *Shabbat*. The only difference is that in the gospels, Jesus gives new meaning to the bread and the wine *– this is my body, this is my blood – broken and shed for us*.

It wasn't a special service with a sample of bread and a sip of wine. It was a real meal with bread and wine, with food and laughter and conversation, and enjoying each other's company. The disciples wouldn't have been solemn – the events of Good Friday had not yet unfolded.

In 1 Corinthians 11:34 Paul chides the Corinthian church for greed and drunkenness. They were coming together for the fellowship meal – a full meal. But some were eating everything before everyone was present and others were getting drunk. Greed and drunkenness not being a great example to others, Paul suggests that, if you are so hungry it makes you bad mannered and greedy, then eat at home. He never said that the meal should be abandoned and reduced down to a religious ritual of a sample of bread and a sip of wine. That is not the thing that Jesus left with the first disciples. He left a meal, in which the bread and wine spoke of his sacrifice on the cross. I am fully convinced that Jesus, ever the partygoer, intended the bread and wine to be shared within a real, natural meal with a few family and friends. I don't believe what we usually do in church services is what Jesus intended.

Now it is true that in a traditional or even informal communion service, one may feel the presence of God or feel close to Jesus. The bread and wine have holy significance however we receive them. My point is that we do not need special robes, or vessels, or tables to *do this in remembrance of* him. He can meet us in a simple meal with family or friends at home. What matters is, are we being intentional? Are we meeting 'in him' or 'in his name' as it were?

So Hil was right in France – he had recognised Jesus in the breaking of the bread. I had not, until he pointed it out. In those natural meals of baguette and *vin rouge*, Jesus had been present as we ate and drank and talked about him.

Martin had a glimpse of the Jewishness of Jesus and how natural a part of the *Shabbat* meal the bread and wine was.

When we have friends to dinner, or at a family meal, we can break bread and pour out wine. It is natural – we don't need to become religious or weird when we do it. If we are intentional, we will meet the Lord in the bread, in the wine, in the conversation, in the laughter, in our thankfulness.

The Lord is here. His Spirit is with us.

'Any intelligent fool can make things bigger, more complex, and more violent. It takes a touch of genius and a lot of courage to move in the opposite direction.'

E.F. Schumacher

fifteen

Re-packing the suitcase

On my early trips to Asia and Africa I took a huge suitcase. I packed every conceivable thing I would need for every conceivable possibility. I had basic hospital equipment, sterilised needles and tubes, drugs for every malady, electrical adapters, power surge protectors, clothes for every occasion, travel laundry items, emergency cash and credit cards incase we got stuck out there longer than expected.

I had photocopies of my passport and the numbers for the British Embassy in all the countries we visited, photocopies of tickets as well as real tickets, emergency biscuits and sweets in case I couldn't eat the food – the list went on and on! And when my case was weighed at the airport, it was not surprisingly, often overweight. And we called these trips 'faith trips'! We rarely had to trust God for anything as we had made provision for every contingency.

What I remember about those trips is that most

of that stuff came back unused every time. It was completely unnecessary. As the years went by, I began to reduce the amount of stuff I took and began just to trust God if anything went wrong.

Today, if God withdrew his Holy Spirit from the church, 99 percent of what happens in church would carry on unchanged. It would carry on because we have planned, prepared, and written the script and outline for the program every time we meet. God rarely gets a look in, and he certainly isn't allowed to lead our meetings very often – we take care of that.

We are carrying so much excess baggage in our churches that we are struggling to even *get to the runway,* let alone take off!

So I have emptied my metaphorical suitcase and bought a much smaller one. Here I want to list a few items I think I'll need. Your list may be different. My list may change as time goes by, but I want to stick with the smaller suitcase.

1. Resting in the love of the Father

The first thing I 'packed' was a resting in God's love. If you don't understand that God loves you just as you are, you'll make little progress. Sure he may love us to a point where we change in certain areas, but let him do that. There is such a culture of performance and competitiveness in the church today that we are giving birth to believers modelled on the elder brother in the story of the lost son – a group of people who are trying to get God's approval by their performance. Yet the story Jesus tells in Luke 15:11 suggests we should be resting in the Father's love like the younger brother. Dad is throwing a party for us. Don't insult him by not enjoying it.

The natural organic way of growth is growth that comes from within the plant or creature. A tree does spring into leaf by a pronouncement from a committee or some human leader. It grows naturally from within as God intended all of us to.

'But when the kindness and love of God our Saviour appeared, he saved us, not because of righteous things we had done, but because of his mercy. He saved us through the washing of rebirth and renewal by the Holy Spirit, whom he poured out on us generously through Jesus Christ our Saviour...' (Titus 3:4-6)

'What the Father showed us in the gift of his Son is that he was unwilling to settle for the indentured servitude of fearful slaves. He preferred instead the intimate affection of sons and daughters.'

Wayne Jacobsen - *He Loves Me!*

2. Trying to live with grace towards other believers.

The new thing, this simple way of 'being the church' that I'm trying, suits me. It may not suit everyone. My way is not superior nor is it inferior to other ways. It is different, that's all.

I have come to see that there is in fact only one church on earth. It is very diverse. Bananas and apples are not the same but they are both fruit. So the diversity of the church isn't helped by one group or sect claiming to be the only true expression of church.

Our local expressions of church should be merely containers of the presence of Jesus. But his message of love and grace always seems too big, too much and too good. We struggle to hold on to it. Perhaps, all together, in all our different ways and expressions of church, just maybe we can hold this Jesus but, even then, probably only part of him.

'So the church is both my greatest intellectual and moral problem and my most consoling home. She is both pathetic whore and frequent bride. There is still a marvelous marriage with such a bride, and many whores do occasionally become brides too. In a certain but real sense, the church itself is the first cross that Jesus is crucified on, as we limit, mangle, and try to control the always too big message. All the churches seem to crucify Jesus again and again by their inability to receive his whole body, but they often resurrect him too. I am without doubt a microcosm of this universal church.'

Richard Rohr - *Falling Upward: A Spirituality for the Two Halves of Life*

3. Believing that the full measure of the Holy Spirit is available all the time, everywhere, to everyone.

Some Christians talk as though we will never see a real work of the Spirit amongst us unless we fast, pray, read our Bible or do all sorts of other stuff. Fasting, praying and other Christian disciplines have a place in discipleship but they have nothing to do with the availability of the Holy Spirit.

I heard a man prophecy over a couple that they were *'living under an open heaven this year.'* I thought to myself, what a strange thing to say. We are all, always living under an open heaven. Heaven opened on the day of Pentecost and the Holy Spirit was poured out on all flesh! Heaven has never closed since!

He is available *everywhere* to *everyone*, *all of the time.* The only condition is that we ask. If we have to go through a fast or a season of deeper prayer or Bible reading before the Holy Spirit shows up, then we have made it all about us and our efforts. Yet the Bible clearly teaches that the coming of the Spirit had nothing to do with us but the Father sent the Holy Spirit as a result of what Jesus did. It is not about us. It is all about him!

'The power of the Spirit cannot be worked up, pulled down, manufactured, or generated by hard work and much praying. The Holy Spirit does not wait till you sweat before giving you his power. Jesus said, 'Ask, and it will be given to you ... Everyone who asks receives' (Mt 7:7-8). Nothing could be simpler!'

Reinhard Bonnke

4. Smell the flowers - Intentionally listening for the voice of Jesus and moving at his much slower pace.

I sometimes wonder what would happen if God banned Christians from using cars. I don't think God is against cars. It is just that we rush around with busy schedules and programs. But Jesus didn't have a car. And there is only one record of him using a donkey. Jesus walked. Let me say that again. Jesus walked. Imagine your church or ministry if everyone walked everywhere. It would be a lot slower wouldn't it? I just cannot see anywhere where Jesus rushed. He was tuned into the voice of his Father all the time. You can hear it in his teaching.

'Consider how the lilies grow.' (Luke 12:27)

Modern life would be difficult if we did walk everywhere but I think I have decided to slow right down in order to hear the voice of the Father more often. I walk much more than I did. I live 20 minutes from town, so I try and walk to the office or meetings nearby.

Jesus seems to teach that we can hear God speaking to us through nature, circumstance, scripture or people. The list may be longer but Jesus walked.

So many of the miracles of healing we read about in the gospels happened on the road when Jesus was walking somewhere. As you reread the gospel, tune into to the slow pace of Jesus. God is not in a rush. He is really slow. Here are a few mentions of Jesus walking. Here is someone who has indeed considered 'how the lilies grow.'

'As Jesus was *walking* beside the Sea of Galilee ...' (Matthew 4:18)

'Jesus left the temple and was *walking* away when his disciples came up to him ...' (Matthew 24:1)

'As he *walked* along, he saw Levi ...' Mark 2:14

'As they were *walking* along the road, a man said to him, "I will follow you wherever you go."' (Luke 9:57)

'and Jesus was in the temple area *walking* in Solomon's Colonnade.' (John 10:23)

5. *Loving the poor*

There are poor people everywhere. In our work at RSVP Trust we spend over £60,000 every year in Africa to help improve life for some of the poorest people in the world. Helping the poor is something the vast majority of people agree on. The Bible teaches that God has a special concern for the poor.

'He who is kind to the poor lends to the Lord, and he will reward him for what he has done.'

(Proverbs 19:17)

In the Early Church there was a concern for the poor that was an integral part of being a disciple of Jesus.

'In Joppa there was a disciple named Tabitha (which, when translated, is Dorcas), who was always doing good and helping the poor.' (Acts 9:36)

When the gospel spread to the non-Jewish world, it came first to a man who helped the poor.

'Cornelius stared at him in fear. 'What is it, Lord?' he asked. The angel answered, 'Your prayers and gifts to the poor have come up as a memorial offering before God.' (Acts 10:4)

The first Apostles had helping the poor high on their agenda.

'All [James, Peter and John] asked was that we should continue to remember the poor, the very thing I was eager to do.' (Galatians 2:10)

'True religion is real living; living with all one's soul, with all one's goodness and righteousness.'

Albert Einstein

I was hungry and you formed a committee to investigate my hunger.

I was homeless and you filed a report on my plight.

I was sick and you held a seminar on the situation of the underprivileged.

You have investigated all the aspects of my plight,

Yet I am still hungry, homeless and sick.

6. Expecting the miraculous

Some things are impossible for we humans. But that does not make them impossible for God. We don't have to work up miracles but coming to any situation with an expectancy for the supernatural seems to cause more miracles to happen.

7. Placing a high value on relationships

I am quite weary of the hierarchical nature of churches where someone uses their position to control, and sometimes even abuse, a church member. As I have studied monastic communities – which I accept may have a loose hierarchy – I have begun to view Christian believers more as a monastic community who live out in the community at large. We are free to follow Christ where he leads. And when we gather together, his Spirit in us teaches the community. I want to be aware of Christ in my friend, in the stranger, in the poor and yes, even in my opponents.

8. Loving and respecting those who are 'other' or 'different'

Every so often, I seem to have a fresh revelation or discover a new vista in my walk with God. Today, some of those people I used to think God had excluded, I see God has included. I don't think God changed. I think I changed. This leads me to conclude that I may change my thinking again as I grow in Christ. There-fore, instead of seeing the world in terms of 'us' and 'them', I chose to see a world of people made in the image of God. Just because some of them are different or 'other' does not make them excluded. I want to show love and respect in the same way I want to be loved and respected.

9. *Maintaining inner quietness*

When I discovered Jesus, I felt bathed in an inner peace. From time to time things happen and disrupt that peace. I believe that the Bible teaches us to let the peace of Christ rule our hearts. By that, I mean that the peace of God is like the referee in a game.

When he blows the whistle the game stops because something was wrong. When I lose my inner peace and become stressed, something is wrong. Sometimes it can be something external, but it often is something in me that is not right. We cannot always control situations in life, but we can control our inner life. When the Spirit blows the whistle, I want to stop and restore my inner peace.

> 'Be anxious for nothing, but in everything by prayer and supplication, with thanksgiving, let your requests be made known to God; and the peace of God, which surpasses all understanding, will guard your hearts and minds through Christ Jesus.' (Philippians 4:6, 7)

There are also certain people and situations that are almost guaranteed to cause me to lose my inner peace – particularly controlling and manipulative people. Sometimes we need to give ourselves strict boundaries and avoid those people and situations where possible, in order to guard our own heart.

> 'Above all else, guard your heart, for it is the wellspring of life.' (Proverbs 4:23)

10. *Intentionally pursuing simplicity*

I used to think everything starts simple by default and we just make it more complicated as we go along.

That is true of some things. But when it comes to the modern day church, I think we started complicated and kept it complicated. Simplicity does not just happen. We have to work to keep things simple.

This was the reason why for a whole year after stopping organised church I refused to start the 'new thing'. It would have so easily have just defaulted to organised church but in a different location, had I jumped in too quick. You really have to work at getting rid of the old before you can put on the new.

So those are the ten things I'm packing in my hand luggage. They may change from time to time. They may become more or fewer as time goes on.

'Jesus is always here. Quietly waiting for us to be still with him and to hear his voice deep within your heart. He is calling you to spend time with him in prayer. But this kind of prayer – real prayer – requires discipline. It requires making time for moments of silence everyday. Often it means waiting for the Lord to speak. In the midst of busyness and the stress of our daily lives we need to make space for silence because it is in silence we find God.'

Pope Benedict XVI

'Unless someone like you cares a whole awful lot, nothing is going to get better. It's not.'

Dr. Seuss

sixteen

Hand luggage

I read this quote recently that really made me think about the cry of a hurting world.

'What scares me is that I'm going to ultimately find out at the end of my life that I'm really not loveable, that I'm not worthy of being loved. That there's something fundamentally wrong with me.'

Demi Moore - Harpers Bazaar -Jan 2012

I really don't think Demi Moore is alone in feeling that way. Society is bubbling with insecurity and fear. We all have the public persona, or Facebook page, that paints what we want everyone else to see and think about us. But the real us, often has a darker, more troubled side that we keep hidden through fear of rejection.

Jesus came with a message of love, which he passed on to his followers. I believe I have encountered that divine love of which he spoke. Yet there is a world out there who think the message of the Christ-followers is *'God is really angry with you. God is really good. You are really bad. You should try harder.'*

We have clearly failed to communicate the good news that while we were yet sinners, Christ loved us and died for us.

Jesus kept bringing the disciples back to love.

'His disciples asked him, 'Rabbi, who sinned, this man or his parents, that he was born blind?' 'Neither this man nor his parents sinned,' said Jesus, 'but this happened so that the work of God might be displayed in his life.' John 9:2, 3

'Then little children were brought to Jesus for him to place his hands on them and pray for them. But the disciples rebuked those who brought them. Jesus said, 'Let the little children come to me, and do not hinder them, for the kingdom of heaven belongs to such as these." (Matthew 19:13, 14)

'A new command I give you: Love one another. As I have loved you, so you must love one another.' (John 13:34)

'But love your enemies, do good to them, and lend to them without expecting to get anything back. Then your reward will be great, and you will be sons of the Most High, because he is kind to the ungrateful and wicked.' Luke 6:35

Jesus taught a new way of living in sharp contrast to the religion of performance of the Pharisees. This lifestyle can be outlined by nine statements:

1. Repent
Jesus first message was 'Repent and believe. The kingdom of heaven is at hand.' Repent means to become thoughtful enough to make some changes.

It is a turning to God. It is not a one time event but a lifestyle of growing spiritually as we learn from our mistakes and faults, and repeatedly turn to God.

2. Believe

Repentance is linked to believing because in turning away from some negative behaviour we know we cannot always help ourselves. An addict may be willing to repent yet unable to change his negative actions by himself. So we need to believe that God loves us, cares for and about us, and can change us. We need to rest in God's love and trust him to do a work in our hearts.

> 'I waited patiently for the LORD;
> he turned to me and heard my cry.
> He lifted me out of the slimy pit,
> out of the mud and mire;
> he set my feet on a rock
> and gave me a firm place to stand.
> He put a new song in my mouth,
> a hymn of praise to our God.'
> (Psalm 40:1-3)

3. Be baptised

To be baptised into Christ is the outward and public sign of a person turning to Jesus. It is a sign that a person has died and risen with Christ in the spirit. It is to identify oneself with Jesus.

4. Love

This command of Jesus is the simplest to understand yet hardest to do. We need God's help to love as Jesus taught. He said our love should be directed in four directions.

a) Love God

We direct our love first to God because putting God

first is the way life works. We love God as we would love anyone else – we think about him, talk to him, have fun with him, seek his embrace when we are sad, confess our wrong actions to him, spend time with him, and sometimes be with him in silence and enjoy his friendship.

b) Love others

Loving God without loving those created in his image doesn't ever work. We are called to love one another, do unto others as we would have them do unto us. We should care for the poor and weak, the least the last and the lost. We should share as much grace as we ourselves would like to receive, if not more.

c) Love yourself

Too many people dislike themselves. If we don't love ourselves, how can we believe that God loves us? Jesus seems to assume that we would love ourselves.

'Love your neighbour as yourself.' (Matthew 22:39)

d) Love your enemy

Jesus goes further than loving God and your pals though. He teaches a new way of living by loving our enemies. He wants to bring an end to the desire for revenge. He points out that the old law *'An eye for and eye and a tooth for a tooth'* was not an encouragement to get revenge. It was a law to prevent revenge from escalating. Revenge always escalates until we end up murdering someone. Therefore God provided a law to say, effectively, that if you lost a tooth, the limit of damages you can claim is one tooth from the perpetrator and no more.

But as ever, in our desire to get revenge we have

turned that limitation of revenge into a 'where there's blame, there's a claim' advert. Jesus says there is a better way. Love your enemies. Don't go for revenge. Go for blessing.

5. Forgive

Forgiveness follows on from loving our enemies but forgiving those who hurt us is not about letting them off the hook. It is about keeping ourselves free. It is about preventing bitterness and anger and hatred from getting a hold in our heart. Forgiving doesn't mean we allow our abuser to keep abusing us. It means setting ourselves free from their control. The abuser will still control part of us if we hold onto to anger and hatred. Not forgiving others is like drinking rat poison ourselves and then expecting the other person to die. It just doesn't work. This is why Jesus told us to live in forgiveness.

6. Pray

To pray is to have a conversation with God. Small children tend to babble while they are learning to talk. The older and wiser we get, the more we listen to others before speaking. We have two ears but only one mouth. There is a hint. Praying is listening for God to speak in our heart and mind. It is about us telling him our concerns, joys and giving thanks.

7. Give

God so loved the world he gave. God is a giver. He gives us each new day and everything we have, eat, drink and enjoy. He wants us to be like him. Something happens when we give to others. Live to give.

8. Remember him in bread and wine

As we have seen, Jesus gave the bread and wine a new meaning at the Last Supper. However we do it, let us remember with thankfulness the giving of his body and blood. We may not understand exactly what happened on that hill outside Jerusalem. But that is what reconnects us with our Father in heaven.

9. Make disciples

This is the one that most Christians struggle with. But it is not about trying to sell a vacuum cleaner to a reluctant customer. It is far more about sharing our real lives and the source of our hope and joy in a natural way. It's sharing life. It's having coffee, a meal, a walk, or a conversation. We don't need a script. We can just be ourselves. It is more about availability and loving others than 'four steps to this or that.'

Nine small words and phrases describing big actions. So simple anyone can understand yet so deep it takes a lifetime to put into action.

If small, loose communities of people began to live this way across the nation and the globe, without the distraction of an institution, the world would be transformed for the better within a year.

Some would argue that organised church keeps us accountable to each other and stops us retreating into comfortable friendship groups. However, I think meeting in small groups, and networks of distant friendships, still keeps us accountable. My aim is not retreating but rather advancing and engaging with reality in a way the institution is not very good at.

Others have asked how those needing help will find these hidden communities? This question ignores the fact that God is involved in people's lives. He can guide people to a group who are seeking to help the needy just as easily as guiding them to a church building.

The Early Church was at its most effective when it was small and loose and open. I believe small, almost monastic, communities could be the hidden revival, going on unnoticed while the institution limps on mostly concerned with itself.

Some ask if the institution and these simple communities are mutually exclusive. I don't think they are necessarily. But if we are trying to be intentionally simple, I think the institution will always get in the way. It has an inherent obsession with controlling things. Bearing in mind that two thirds of Christians live their faith outside the institution of organised church, I am not sure what relevance the institution has to most people's lives.

When I was growing up there were clear lines of authority – the police, anyone in a uniform, the teacher, any grown up, our parents. Society was ordered that way. In that sort of organised authoritarian society, the hierarchy of the church worked. The bishops and clergy were seen as part of that arrangement.

Today we live in a very different society, one that has the hallmark of social networks like Facebook and Twitter. On those sites, everyone's opinions and comments carry the same weight. The internet itself has no boss, no president and no one in overall control. It was designed to be like that. It is in many ways a reflection of the globalisation our lives. The upcoming generation rarely sit through uninterrupted monologues but exchange quick-fire conversation through 140 character status updates. They don't recognise the old authority structures.

In this sort of *'always on'*, socially networked society, the old church institution creaks and looks evermore irrelevant. While some people cling to the old rugged church, Jesus is mostly encountered elsewhere, usually at street level. And that is where I want to be.

'Then the disciples went out and preached everywhere, and the Lord worked with them and confirmed his word by the signs that accompanied it.'

(Mark 16:20)

Suggested reading

A million miles in a thousand years - Donald Miller

Blue like jazz - Donald Miller

Divine Nobodies - Jim Palmer

Evolving in Monkey Town - Rachel Held Evans

Introverts in the Church - Adam S McHugh

Pagan Christianity - Frank Viola & George Barna

Reimagining Church - Frank A Viola

Searching for God knows what - Donald Miller

So you don't want to go to church anymore? - Wayne Jacobsen & Dave Coleman

The Parables of Grace - Robert Farrar Capon

The Ragamuffin Gospel - Brennan Manning

The Shack - William P Young

Traveling Mercies - Anne Lamott

Wide open spaces - Jim Palmer

About the author

Don Egan is a Christian speaker and the author of *The Chronicles of Godfrey, Searching For Home, Healing is Coming, Beautiful On The Mountains* and *Spiritual Detox* along with several other books.

He is the founder of RSVP Trust, a Registered Charity that transforms the lives of people in the UK and Africa.

He lives in Suffolk UK and has spoken to thousands of people in public in the UK, Africa and Asia over the last 30 years.

To contact Don please visit *www.rsvptrust.co.uk*.

Twitter: @Don_Egan

Printed in Great Britain
by Amazon

36891501R00086